W9-CBG-526

728 Nolan, David
NOL

    The houses of St. Augustine

SEP 11 '96

DATE DUE			
DEC 30 01			
AUG - 6 2002			
AUG 2 4 2002			

THE HOUSES OF
ST. AUGUSTINE

31 ST. FRANCIS STREET

David Nolan

30 & 28 MARINE STREET

Paintings by Jean Ellen Fitzpatrick
Photographs by Ken Barrett, Jr.

The Houses of St. Augustine

20 Valencia Street

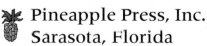

Pineapple Press, Inc.
Sarasota, Florida

MARTIN COUNTY LIBRARY SYSTEM
701 EAST OCEAN BLVD.
STUART, FLORIDA 34994-2374

Text copyright ©1995 by David Nolan
Paintings copyright © 1995 Jean Ellen Fitzpatrick
Photographs (except as otherwise noted) © 1995 Ken Barrett, Jr.
All rights reserved. No part of this book may be reproduced in any form or
by any means, electronic or mechanical, including photocopying, recording,
or by any information storage and retrieval system, without permission in
writing from the publisher.

Inquiries should be addressed to:
Pineapple Press, Inc.
P.O. Drawer 16008
Southside Station
Sarasota, Florida 34239

The poem "Houses," reprinted in the Epilogue, copyright 1926 by the
Century Company, from *Taxis and Toadstools* by Rachel Field. Used by
Permission of Bantam Doubleday Dell Books for Young Readers.

Library of Congress Cataloging in Publication Data

Nolan, David, 1946–
    The houses of St. Augustine/by David Nolan : paintings by Jean Ellen
Fitzpatrick : photographs by Ken Barrett, Jr.—1st ed.
        p.   cm.
    Includes bibliographical references and index.
    ISBN 1-56164-069-7.—ISBN 1-56164-075-1 (pbk.)
    1. Architecture, Domestic—Florida—Saint Augustine—Pictorial works.
2. Historic buildings—Florida—Saint Augustine—Pictorial works.   3. Saint
Augustine (Fla.)   I. Title.
NA7238.S27N65   1995   94-41776
728′.09759′18-dc20   CIP

First Edition
10   9   8   7   6   5   4   3   2   1

Design by Octavo Design & Production, Inc., and Jean Ellen Fitzpatrick
Printed in Hong Kong by Oceanic Graphics

CONTENTS

44 AVENIDA MENENDEZ

42 SPANISH STREET

14 ST. FRANCIS STREET

47 MARINE STREET

33 AVILES STREET

38 SOUTH DIXIE HIGHWAY

28 SARAGOSSA STREET

268 ST. GEORGE STREET

1636 MASTERS DRIVE

22 AVENIDA MENENDEZ

70 WATER STREET

66 PARK PLACE

20 NELMAR AVENUE

Playing Sherlock Holmes with Historic Buildings

OPEN THE DOORS

"There is one enormous source of artistic pleasure of which too few are as yet aware; there is one art whose works confront us wherever man lives, which all too many of us daily pass blindly by. That source is to be found in the buildings all around us; that art is the art of architecture."

Talbot F. Hamlin, 1947

IN 1977 I MOVED TO ST. AUGUSTINE, FLORIDA, the nation's oldest city, along with my wife and year-old daughter. I had in my bank account the savings from a decade of various jobs, and planned to write a book.

I thought it was all worked out, but had reckoned without inflation, so after nine months I was looking for a job.

As luck would have it, just at that time there was an advertisement in the newspaper saying that the Historic St. Augustine Preservation Board was looking for someone to work on a survey of old buildings.

Architecture and history have been my passions ever since childhood, so it seemed like a good match. I spent the next two years walking up and down every street of the Ancient City, stopping in front of almost every house and filling out a form listing everything from roof style to foundation material.

It caused me to look sharply at details as never before. To this day, I cannot pass an interesting building without making note of the style of its windows (speculating on whether or not they have been changed over the years), or its decorative elements, or other features that might previously have merged into one generalized, overall impression. I have learned the delight of details, as well as some of their meanings,

52 ST. GEORGE STREET 46 BRIDGE STREET

and if this book can pass them on to you, then it will not have been a labor in vain.

As I walked the streets, through hot summers and occasionally (despite the fact that this is Florida) brisk winters, getting soaked by flash showers, leaping out of the way of speeding automobiles, periodically being buzzed by yellow flies or attacked by mosquitoes, and putting holes through the soles of four pairs of shoes, I occupied my mind by endlessly asking the question "Why?" Why was this building in this particular

36 CORDOVA STREET

85 Bridge Street

99 Kelley Lane

42 Spanish Street

32 SEVILLA STREET

location? Why did it look the way it did? What changes had been made to it over the years? I also asked—because I truly love and care about this historic place—what could be done now to bring out the best in it: the house, the neighborhood, and the city itself? I puzzled over the answers, street by street and house by house, from one end of town to the other.

The answers, of course, did not just come out of my head. I ransacked libraries for books and publications on architecture and history. I cranked through miles of microfilm of old newspapers, letting out cheers when I would come across an article about the building of a house that I had just seen on the street, comfortably (or sometimes distressingly) settled into its sixth or seventh decade of existence.

We had a good set of maps from which we could date the houses within a range of years. Most useful were the Sanborn Fire Insurance Maps, produced for St. Augustine in 1884, 1888, 1893, 1899, 1904, 1910, 1917, 1924, and 1930. They showed the outline of every building, its construction materials, number of stories, and the like.

For buildings of the past century, you could take the maps in sequence and see where the site was once a vacant lot, then note when a structure first appeared, then follow through on later maps to see what enlargements had been made.

23 SEVILLA STREET

The Sanborn mapmakers may have thought they were just doing something to benefit the insurance industry, but in fact their greatest contribution was to history—by providing the kind of details, not just for St. Augustine, but for towns and cities all over the country, that are nowhere else as immediately accessible. To anyone restoring or researching an old house, the Sanborn maps are a treasure trove of information. Woe be to the restorer who pounds the first nail or pries off the first board without carefully consulting them.

(This reminds me of a time when two entrepreneurs developing a fancy restaurant called me in to tell them something about their building. "The two most outstanding things, architecturally," I told them, "are the front windows that run almost floor to ceiling, and the shutters that go with them." Their faces dropped. "We just carted them to the dump," they wailed. Let that be a warning!)

Not as frequent in their coverage over the years, but even more interesting for the art that went into them, were the bird's-eye view maps of St. Augustine produced in 1885 and 1894. Bird's-eyes were a popular 19th-century art form linked to the promotion of real estate. Itinerant mapmakers would travel the country, making grid plans of the town or city, then sketching in every single building as if seen from a low-flying plane—except that airplanes hadn't been invented yet.

The ones done of St. Augustine are of amazingly high quality. If they show a building having two windows across the front, then that building had two windows. I know: I checked them more carefully than any but the most obsessed collector of bird's-eyes possibly could. It's no accident that our office periodically rang out with the shout, "Thank God for the bird's-eyes!" We only wished there had been more of them.

They gave us the only pictorial record of most of our old buildings, since photographers, then and now, have a lamentable tendency to stick to the tourist route and give us thousands of pictures of the same handful of buildings.

That is not to say we did not also sing the praises of photographers past—both the professionals who came here during the Civil War and after, and the amateurs who captured their vacations or their family homes. Some of their work appears in this book to give a sense of how buildings have changed over the years.

39 VALENCIA STREET

17 CINCINNATI AVENUE

181 CORDOVA STREET

Postcards, too, yielded up their various views, and went into the mix that gave us a visual look at times gone by.

Some of the praise that went to the diligent makers of bird's-eye and Sanborn maps should also go to the low-paid compilers of city directories. These volumes are another indispensable weapon in the arsenal of the old-house historian. They tell who lived in a building, along with their family status, race, and occupation. For a few hundred of the most interesting places, we traced the records back nearly a century. We sometimes found gems like 20 Valencia Street, which served as retirement home for not one, but two Union generals from the Civil War—in this very Southern town.

There were also legal records to go through at the county courthouse—a process made much easier when the local abstract company let us use their indexes. We frequently ran into that bane of researchers, the assertion that old records had disappeared. In some cases this was undoubtedly true, as I have occasionally seen

124 MARINE STREET   172 AVENIDA MENENDEZ

old city and county records for sale at antique and junk shops. But there was also, inevitably, the feeling that some records deemed vanished were in fact stored up in the towers of the courthouse in an area inhabited by musty cartons and live pigeons—and the people of whom the request was made did not want to consider the hike and filth as falling within the purview of their job descriptions.

Building permits in many cities are meticulously kept and a wonderful source of information about the age of buildings and the improvements made thereon. Alas, those too were among the records—at least of the vintage we sought—that were said to be "gone with the wind."

Beyond the documentary records are the oral recollections of those who lived in particular buildings or neighborhoods. They are potentially the most fruitful source of information, though not without occasional pitfalls.

I ran into these in interesting ways. As I stopped in front of the houses, filling out forms, people naturally assumed I was the property appraiser, there to raise their taxes. They came charging out and cursed me accordingly.

Once their anger had been vented, I explained that I was not a property appraiser, but rather a house detective. I wondered if they could tell me anything about the history of their building. Then the stories started to pour forth. One woman recalled watching the huge

6 VALENCIA STREET

41 SAN MARCO AVENUE

400 OLD QUARRY ROAD

1913 funeral of Henry Flagler, the great Florida developer, from the very porch where we sat talking. And she told me how Dr. John Harvey Kellogg, the inventor of breakfast cereal and peanut butter, had rented a cottage in the backyard from her father. Others pointed out where buildings had been moved. One showed me where Al Capone stayed in St. Augustine. These were just some of the highlights that had never been recorded before. I have, ever since, pitied historians who don't have time to talk to people.

Of course, there are *caveats*: recollections of dates can be off by decades, and some tales can be stretched taller than the proverbial India-rubber man. The trick, as in any research, is to check and double check.

There is an additional hazard in a city like St. Augustine, where a building's age has been so closely linked with its commercial and real estate value. It was not uncommon for a quick century to be added to the date of construction. Before our survey was done, no one had ever attempted to date the Ancient City's buildings, except for a handful of colonial ones. After we finished, the results were not always wildly embraced, and some of the most outrageous tall tales continue to flourish.

I remember one woman who was opening a bed-and-breakfast inn and asked me to help her find out about the building it occupied. I launched her on a search through a long shelf of city directories and showed her how to trace the house and its residents. Five minutes later she came back in disgust.

"That's too much work," she said. "If I could just get a good ghost story to tell about the place. . ."

So, welcome to St. Augustine, where history has been coined into gold and sometimes falsified accordingly. A few untruths have been around so long that they have acquired a distinction of their own as folklore. Others will, I hope, be corrected so that the twains of what is said and what actually happened may someday meet.

I also hope that those who live in the Ancient City, as well as those who visit here, will be enabled by this book to look with a more interested and informed eye on the architectural and historic treasures that line our streets.

Most of all, I hope that everyone will have the politeness of a junkyard dog the next time someone suggests demolishing yet another of our old buildings for a parking lot, gas station, or fast-food joint.

Gr-r-r-r-r-r-r-r-r-r!!!

9 CARRERA STREET

CHAPTER ONE
The Colonial Period

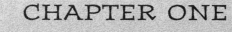

MARINE STREET LOOKING SOUTH FROM BRIDGE STREET

The block-long section of Marine Street between Bridge and
St. Francis Streets contains one of the finest collections of colonial buildings in the city. They were constructed before the seawall on the bayfront, and thus cling to the Marine Street rather
than the Avenida Menendez side of their building lots. Buildings
closer to the water tend to date from the Flagler era when the
seawall was safely in place to protect them from periodic inun-
dation. Several of the houses on Marine Street were occupied in
early years by the black children of well-to-do white men.

MANY PLACES THAT CATER TO the tourist trade have their Olde-this or Olde-that, but in St. Augustine that antiquated spelling gives way to the more assertive "Oldest"—drawing on the city's distinction as the oldest continuous European settlement in the continental United States. It dates its origin to 1565 and hails as its founder the Spanish conquistador Pedro Menéndez de Avilés.

The city's survival is in many ways a miracle. It lacked the gold and silver that made other areas to the south crown jewels in the Spanish Empire. The justification for its continuance over the years was that as a military outpost it provided some protection to the treasure fleets bringing wealth from the other colonies to Spain.

The city lasted more than three centuries before a viable method was found of dealing with the dreaded yellow fever. Early colonial correspondence is an endless complaint of poverty, late subsidies, hardship, and threat of attack. Not just threat: periodically through the years it was sacked and looted and burned. St. Augustine's history is punctuated by the names of invaders—widely known, notorious, or forgotten. Sir Francis Drake in 1586, Robert Searles in 1668, Governor James Moore of Carolina in 1702, and General James Oglethorpe of Georgia in 1740, all left their scorch marks on the Ancient City.

Some of these were sheer piracy, but most drew their justification from the international power politics of the age. St. Augustine was born of the conflict between France and Spain, and later attacked and reinforced as a result of centuries of struggle and ill will between England and Spain. For two decades it even flew the British flag, remaining a loyal fourteenth colony during the American Revolution and serving as a place of detention for three signers of the Declaration of Independence. It switched back to Spanish rule as part of the international settlement of that conflict.

Volumes and volumes could be, and have been, written of this history, still only scratching the surface in many areas. Here we are concerned primarily with the architectural record: both what remains and what has vanished.

Much, of course, has disappeared. War, hurricane, humid climate, hungry termites, and human folly (powered by technological advances as the centuries have gone by) all contributed their part. The modern city can boast parking lots, office buildings, and an endless array of T-shirt shops where colonial structures once stood.

For those buildings that survived into the era of photography—dating from the Civil War and after—we have some record as to their appearance, albeit with the alterations of decades or centuries.

For those destroyed before that time, our major sources are the art of conjecture matched with the shapes and fragments dug up by archaeologists, the legal descriptions designed in one way or another to tax properties for the king's coffers, and the occasional—and sometimes conflicting—descriptions of travelers.

There are a few extant artists' renditions, but the earliest of these are so fanciful as to show mountains ringing the ever-flat St. Augustine landscape, thus calling into question the veracity of other details as well.

No building survives from the 1500s. The archaeologists paint a picture of flimsy structures of wattle-and-daub or rude boards, unlikely to have survived just the time, much less the hardships, the area endured.

From the 1600s we have only our most enduring landmark, the Castillo de San Marcos, a masonry fort constructed between 1672 and 1695 (with, of course, many later revisions). The masonry used is the native shellstone called coquina. A shell aggregate, mostly of the miniature clamlike *donax*, it is found in coastal regions of Florida, Cuba, and Spain—though often in a form closer in consistency to sand than to stone. Only in certain areas is it solid enough to be quarried for building purposes. One of the finest types is called the Anastasia Formation, a serviceable bed running down the island that is separated from St. Augustine by the Matanzas River.

It is of this material that all but one of the surviving colonial buildings of St. Augustine are made: a tribute more to its greater durability than to an original dominance in numbers. In colonial times, wooden buildings were probably as numerous as coquina ones; they have just met an unkinder fate over the years.

Another type of masonry widely used in colonial times was tabby, which made use of the locally plentiful oyster shells. These, mixed with lime, sand, and water were poured and tamped into wooden forms

The Three Oldest Houses

"First, we went to St. George Street and visited the oldest house in the United States. Then we went to Hospital Street and seen the oldest house in the United States. Then we turned the corner and went down St. Francis Street and inspected the oldest house in the United States. . . ."

When Ring Lardner had the fictional character in his 1917 story "Gullible's Travels" thus recount his sojourn in the Ancient City, some people thought he was merely twitting us for our tendency to have an "oldest" everything. But, in fact, there were at that time three competing oldest houses, at the locations listed. The situation was resolved when the St. Augustine Historical Society acquired all three, closed down two, and settled on 14 St. Francis Street as the oldest house (though in recent years they have downplayed that as its sole claim to fame and operated it as a house museum depicting various eras in St. Augustine history). It is difficult to say which is really our oldest house because of the absence of land records from the First Spanish Period. (Some were destroyed by fire, and the location of the rest is unknown.)

The society did make an appropriate selection from among the three contenders, however. Dodge's Oldest House at 54 St. George Street, which was billed as dating from 1565, was in fact built in the early 1800s. Whitney's Oldest House at 36 Aviles (formerly Hospital) Street, which claimed a date of 1516, likewise dates from the 1800s. The Historical Society's Oldest House, at least, dates from the century prior to that.

36 AVILES STREET

Whitney's Oldest House at 36 Aviles Street was one of the enterprises of a colorful post Civil War developer of Ancient City attractions named John Whitney. A relative of Eli Whitney and friend of Mrs. Abraham Lincoln, he "discovered" the first fountain of youth, off Masters Drive, in the 1870s. He also dabbled in journalism, real estate, and spiritualism. His son ran an alligator farm. 36 Aviles was owned by free blacks during much of the 19th century, prior to its incarnation as an oldest house.

14 ST. FRANCIS STREET

14 St. Francis Street (above) as it appeared decked out in Victorian garb at the turn of the century, with turret, patterned shinglework, eyebrow dormer, and an impressive coquina tower decorated with shells. This is rather my favorite view of the old place. Also shown (right) is a view of the same building at the end of the century, after 75 years of stewardship by the St. Augustine Historical Society.

until dry. Other coastal cities have impressive tabby buildings, but here they proved to have short lifespans and left scant remains—the most visible being a section of wall between 214 St. George Street and the parking lot next door.

There are only about 35 surviving colonial buildings in the Ancient City. The exact number varies depending on definition. If a building contains a few colonial stones but was otherwise constructed in the 1930s (as is the case with Government House on the downtown Plaza), is it colonial? Or if, like the Worth House on the bayfront, it is composed of old material but was within recent memory dismantled stone by stone and moved across the street, does that count as being of new or ancient vintage?

For a few others, it has not yet been possible to pinpoint, from the documentary record, whether they were built in late colonial or early American times, though this has seldom hindered the owners from claiming the more antique time of origin.

There may even be some as-yet-undiscovered colonial buildings. The survey we conducted between 1978 and 1980 added five to the hitherto locally accepted list, and since that time another was almost simultaneously discovered and demolished at—of all places—the St. Augustine Airport.

That was the old Casa Cola plantation house on the North River, associated historically with the Sabate family, and used during part of this century as a dairy farm by the Florida School for the Deaf and the Blind.

It had been remodeled to appear as a 1920s-vintage bungalow. However, as a bulldozer's blade bit into it in 1987 to clear the property for airport expansion, an ancient coquina wall was uncovered, creating a flurry of excitement among historians and archaeologists who rushed to document and preserve it.

Alas, just days later a bulldozer mysteriously and bizarrely leveled it, the malefactor immediately making off, not to be seen in these parts again. The archaeologists had some fine ruins to dig amongst, and the airport was not troubled by any inconvenient old buildings on its property.

As penance for its dereliction of stewardship, the Airport Authority put up $3,000 to study the property, and the final report concluded that the vanished structure—presumed to be the last of what was (before the

Before . . .

214 ST. GEORGE STREET
What is said to be the last free-standing tabby wall from the First Spanish Period is visible on the lower right of the above photo. Coquina stone blocks can be seen to the left of it. This important colonial remnant is perched precariously between 214 St. George Street and a neighboring parking lot.

. . . and after

CASA COLA PLANTATION HOUSE

Alice in Wonderland

Lowered to 1 story during the Flagler Era.

After the Civil War (right front) at 2 ¹/₂ stories.

In 1911 it gained a shingled second story.

The famous arches on the bayfront side.

44 AVENIDA MENENDEZ

The building at 44 Avenida Menendez is the architectural equivalent of the title character in *Alice in Wonderland,* who alternately grew and shrank. It had plenty of time in which to do it: at least part of the house was built during the First Spanish Period, and thus it is one of the very oldest in the city.

Originally one story high, it gained a coquina second story in the 1790s. A photo taken after the Civil War shows it with two and a half stories, with dormer windows. Then it came down to one story and was used as an outbuilding for coal, wood, and storage, serving an elegant mansion built on the bayfront side of the property. It managed to survive the 1887 fire that decimated downtown, though its roof may have burned off in the conflagration. New owners in 1911 added a shingled second story with balcony and rented it out as apartments. In 1914 another fire struck and reduced the new addition to ashes. The old walls were remodeled for a garage, with living quarters attached.

In 1965, as part of the restoration effort, the building was remodeled to serve as an accountant's office. This house once had some of the most ornate coquina work found locally around its Charlotte Street doorway; unfortunately this was not among the features restored. Most amazing, perhaps, is that the arches, which are the town's most outstanding, managed to survive all these fires and remodelings, contractions and enlargements. They merit a close look as a classic of the St. Augustine style.

35 MARINE STREET

FREE BLACK HOUSE   In St. Augustine, where the age of so many buildings has been exaggerated, there is a real oddity in the building at 35 Marine Street. It is an authentic colonial building whose exterior has been remodeled to blend in with the modern motel to which it is attached.

Parts of this building may even date back to the First Spanish period, making it one of the very oldest in town—though the definitive research to prove that has not yet been done.

Of particular interest is the racial history of this house. In 1811 it was traded for a slave woman and her child, but by 1821 it was owned by a free black woman named Chloe Ferguson. The Ferguson family lived here until the Civil War, and then another free black woman, Hager Carr, occupied it until her death at the end of the century. In the early 20th century it was used to house the butler, chauffeur, and gardener for a mansion that was built on the waterfront side of the property. This house has seen a lot of history, but has yet to disgorge its secrets.

Seminole War of 1835–42) a string of plantations along the North River—was of late colonial vintage.

Colonial buildings in St. Augustine need not predate 1776. The Ancient City's period of colonial rule continued until a July day in 1821 when the American flag was raised and the Spanish flag lowered over the Castillo de San Marcos.

St. Augustine's colonial history, like Julius Caesar's Gaul, can be divided into three parts. We refer to these periods, in historical shorthand, as First Spanish (1565–1763), British (1764–1784), and Second Spanish (1784–1821).

There are perhaps ten buildings surviving from the First Spanish Period, none, except the Castillo, predating 1700. This is due to a particularly incendiary raid by Governor Moore of Carolina in 1702 when almost everything in the city except the fort was reported to have been burned. Pinning an exact date on the surviving buildings from the 1700s is difficult because the land records from the First Spanish Period were long ago evacuated from St. Augustine and never returned. They are one of the treasure troves that historians yet hope to find and bring back, and their discovery will be the occasion for new research on our earliest surviving houses.

One of the most significant building projects of the First Spanish Period—destined to have vast reverberations in American history—was the construction of Fort Mose in 1738. Its importance derives from the fact that it was the first legally sanctioned community of freed slaves in this country, and thus an important harbinger of things to come.

As the English began settling—or, to the Spanish mind, encroaching on—land north of Florida, they established a plantation economy based on slave labor. Some of the more spirited slaves would escape through the first "underground railroad," which led to Spanish Florida. There they were given sanctuary. Their numbers grew to such a point that the Spaniards incorporated them into their defense plans. Figuring, rightly, that none would have as much stake in resisting British invasion as those who had already tasted, and escaped from, British slavery, they built Gracia Real de Santa Teresa de Mose on the northern defense line of the city in 1738. The first fort was evacuated at the time of Oglethorpe's raid in 1740, but a second one was built in the 1750s, and the community there survived until the British gained control of Florida by the 1763 Treaty of Paris. Mose residents left with the Spanish and established a similar community in Cuba.

The British, during the two decades they ruled the Ancient City, attempted to develop plantations, as they had done with their colonies to the north. The British left their architectural mark mostly in the remodeling of buildings. To the Spanish structures they inherited, they added second stories, chimneys, window glass, exterior shutters, and doors that provided access directly into the houses, rather than taking people first through an open loggia overlooking the inside of the compound. We know of only one building dating entirely from the British Period: the King's Bakery, which was turned into a garage for the Florida National Guard in the 1930s. Some of the wooden

214 St. George Street

214 St. George Street is one of the handful of buildings dating to the First Spanish Period. Under British rule it was home to the controversial Dr. Robert Catherwood, condemned by a fellow physician as "a bad apothecary who rose to be a worse surgeon." He didn't rank much better as a public servant; he was suspended from office in 1783 on charges of speculating in captured slaves and charging extortionate fees for justice. During the Flagler era, this building housed the Women's Exchange, which raised money by selling jellies and needlework and renting rooms "especially adapted for ladies coming alone and wishing a central yet quiet place." In the 1960s it served as a real estate office for an uncle of President John F. Kennedy. The owners of this and the neighboring Moeller House at 224 St. George Street spearheaded a campaign to keep a multilevel parking facility from being sandwiched between the two colonial houses in 1993.

"One very pretty feature of the houses here struck me agreeably. There is oftentimes a sort of shaded walk under half the house, opening upon the garden. You go up a dusty street, and stand at a door, which you expect will open into a hall. It opens, and a garden full of flowers and trees meets your view. The surprise is delightful."

—Harriet Beecher Stowe,
Palmetto Leaves (1873)

143 St. George Street

143 St. George Street was built in the First Spanish Period as home of the Royal Treasurer. During the British Period it housed Lieutenant Governor John Moultrie (whose brother was an American general during the Revolutionary War that rent the family asunder). As the British prepared to leave in 1784, Governor Patrick Tonyn made his home here. In the Second Spanish Period the building was vacant for a time, and then used to house slaves. An 1821 description said that the house "at the present time consists of some walls of stone covered with shingles and very deteriorated." In 1837 it was purchased by Dr. Seth Peck, who had settled here after practicing medicine in upstate New York. He fancied the place up and added the wooden second floor. It served three generations of the Peck family for nearly a century. Poet Sidney Lanier (1842–1881) was once a guest here. In 1931 Miss Anna Burt, the last of the Peck family, left the house to the city of St. Augustine, along with furnishings, artwork, and an endowment, to be maintained "as an example of the old ante-bellum homes of the South, without substantial change." The city at first rejected the gift, but finally accepted it when the Women's Exchange agreed to take charge. They opened it to the public in 1932. A major restoration project from 1968-1970 included reconstruction of the east wing, returning the house to its earlier U-shape.

7 Bridge Street

7 Bridge Street is a fine example of Second Spanish Period architecture, built in the early 1800s. The mother of Jacksonville's first mayor lived here. It is best known for its century-long connection with the Sanchez family, whose members christened it Bleak House, after the novel by Charles Dickens. This house was the focus of restoration efforts during the 1930s.

Levittown, 1800

Pattern houses that look alike are not strictly a modern phenomenon. We have Victorian examples of them at the east end of Rohde Avenue and the west end of Carrera Street. And, this being the Oldest City, we can even go back to colonial times: there are three houses in a one-block area of Aviles Street that were all basically alike, though they have been remodeled differently over the years. They offer a unique opportunity for studying cookie-cutter housing in one of its early incarnations. 12, 20, and 21 Aviles Street, all $2\frac{1}{2}$-story hip-roofed coquina houses with loggias and balconies built about 1800, proceeded to go their separate—but by no means uninteresting—ways.

Photo courtesy of St. Augustine Historical Society

Number 12, built for a prominent Minorcan family, the Seguis, was later the boyhood home (if not, as is sometimes claimed, the birthplace) of Edmund Kirby Smith, the last Confederate general to surrender. For nearly a century it was the public library (under the presidency, during World War II, of Marjorie Kinnan Rawlings), sharing space with a courtroom, a newspaper office, and the Daughters of the American Revolution. It entered its second library century in 1995, serving the St. Augustine Historical Society.

Number 20, next door, may have been the Ancient City's first bookstore; at least the first owner sold schoolbooks there, along with groceries and liquor. It is most famous as a boarding house, a first-class establishment before the age of the great hotels. Constance Fenimore Woolson, the novelist and unrequited lover of Henry James, was among the guests. It is called the Fatio House, after Miss Louisa Fatio who ran it before and after the Civil War. It was the birthplace of the St. Augustine Art Association, and, as part of the restoration efforts of the 1930s, it was acquired by the Colonial Dames, who have cared for it ever since. The picture shown here depicts it on the eve of their takeover. The photograph is by the legendary architectural photographer Frances Benjamin Johnston (1864–1952), who took it in 1937, before the Christmas decorations had been removed.

Number 21, across the street, was built for Manuel Solana, a member of one of the antique Spanish families. After the Civil War it was purchased by Dr. Oliver Bronson, a New York physician who became St. Augustine's largest taxpayer and one of its leading benefactors. He oversaw the founding of the Buckingham Smith Benevolent Association to benefit the black people of the city, among other charitable ventures. Charles Hamblen, the next owner, made his fortune selling hardware and building materials during the Flagler boom. The local society journal hailed the residence of this transplanted Mainer as "a representative old Spanish house, that at the same time affords a delightful modern home." In the early 20th century it served as a meeting place for most of the labor unions in St. Augustine, from brick masons and cigar makers to plumbers and printing pressmen. It housed the obligatory real estate office during the 1920s boom (as did the Fatio House across the street). Curios, sheet music, and antiques were peddled from it in later decades, until it became a bed-and-breakfast inn in the 1980s. The arches of its loggia may be compared with those at 12 Aviles in the old photos here. Alas, in recent decades the Solana arches have been enclosed.

The Minorcan Colonists

"... they settled in St. Augustine; where their descendants form a numerous, industrious and virtuous body of people, distinct alike from the indolent character of the Spaniard and the rapacious habits of some of the strangers who have visited that city since the exchange of flags. In their duties as small farmers, hunters, fishermen, and other laborious but useful occupations, they contribute more to the real stability of society than any other class of people: generally temperate in their mode of life, and strict in their moral integrity, they do not yield the palm to the denizens of the land of steady habits: crime is almost unknown among them; speaking their native tongue, they move about distinguished by a primitive simplicity and honesty, as remarkable as their speech."

—Charles Vignoles,
Observations Upon the Floridas (1823)

his 1926 novel *Spanish Bayonet*. The author's great-grandfather, Pedro Benet, known as "King of the Minorcans," was a lifelong St. Augustine resident.

With the change of flags over the Ancient City, typically most of the residents evacuated: when the British came, the Spanish left; when the Spanish returned, the British left; when the Americans came, the Spanish left. But the Minorcans stayed, regardless of which flag flew over the fort, and thus acquired an almost unmatched longevity in the city. The closest group to which they might be compared in distinctiveness is the Cajuns of Louisiana.

It is from the Second Spanish Period (1784–1821) that most of the surviving colonial buildings—about two dozen—date.

The visitor to St. George Street will perhaps be puzzled by these small numbers. How to tally them with the vista of balconies and ancient-appearing structures that line the street? The answer, of course, is that many of them are fake—the result of a program of remodeling and reconstruction inspired by Colonial Williamsburg and launched locally in the 1930s as an answer to the economic hardships of the Great Depression. The process went into abeyance with the onset of World War II, then returned in new and larger forms in the late 1950s. It has left its mark on the city, a tale that will be told, more appropriately, later on.

houses constructed during that time were dismantled for transportation to the Bahamas when the British withdrew in 1784. Also shipped to the Bahamas was the Ancient City's first printing press (a well-traveled one, since it had previously been in Charleston), which had produced the state's pioneer newspaper, *The East-Florida Gazette*, in 1783.

The greatest remnant of the British Period was not in buildings but in people. The most ambitious of the development schemes of that time was the plan of Dr. Andrew Turnbull to establish an indigo plantation at New Smyrna, 70 miles south of St. Augustine, and import large numbers of indentured laborers from the Mediterranean to work it. Some were Greek, some Italian, but the largest group were from the island of Minorca in the Balearics east of Spain, and all of the colonists (and their descendants) have come, over the years, to be called Minorcans. The conditions at New Smyrna were horrendous, and in 1777 the colonists, under the leadership of Francisco Pellicer, marched to St. Augustine, where they were given sanctuary by the governor, and settled an area on north St. George Street known as the Minorcan Quarter—the heart of the modern-day tourist area. The dramatic story of the Minorcans was told by Stephen Vincent Benét in

Colonial Details

The oldest colonial remnant in St. Augustine is not a house or a public building, but rather the layout of the town itself. Among other "firsts," it may lay claim to being the first planned city in the country. Its founding date of 1565 was within a decade of the promulgation by King Philip II of Spain of the landmark 1573 ordinances on the planning of new cities.

Over the centuries, and particularly in the automobile age, the narrow streets of the city have given rise to many curses and efforts to widen. But to do so would be to destroy part of the earliest surviving remnant of the Spanish settlement.

Rising up from the historic grid plan of the city are the built details that, with all their changes over the years, combine to give the distinctive look that differentiates St. Augustine from most other American cities. The houses are built right to the street line. In the early

The 1573 Spanish regulations on laying out new towns affected the way St. Augustine developed, even though no buildings from those earliest years survive. Here is a summation of some of the applicable points whose results can still be seen:

- The town should start at the plaza. In coastal areas this should be near the landing.

- A length equal to at least one and one-half widths is recommended for plazas where fiestas using horses are held.

- The corners of the plaza should face the four principal winds, because then the streets running from the plaza will be protected from the unpleasant effects of the winds.

- No lots on the plaza should be assigned to private individuals. They should be used for church and government.

- Houses should be oriented to take advantage of the north and south winds. They should be arranged so they can double as defense barriers, and should have yards and corrals for horses and work animals.

- The cathedral should be visible from the ocean and should be able to serve defensive purposes.

- Buildings should be in the same style for the sake of beauty.

43 CORDOVA STREET

days they had an almost fortified aspect: windows along the street were protected with grilled *rejas* (a colonial version of burglar bars), and heavy gates in high walls provided access to the property. In later years, with changing tastes and styles and levels of danger, doorways appeared right on the street—one of the major architectural changes of the British Period, along with glass windows and exterior shutters which replaced the earlier *rejas*.

While there is a vogue, nowadays, for exposed coquina walls, the colonial builder would have been appalled at this foolishness. The porous stone is truly excellent at conducting moisture, and, to prevent this, it was invariably plastered on the outside to provide a degree of waterproofing. The plaster was sometimes finished in ashlar scoring to make it appear as if the building had been constructed

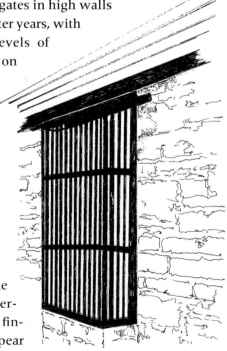

Reja.

of large, carefully cut stones rather than the random rubblework that often lay hidden beneath.

In a rainstorm (with which Florida is usually amply blessed), the streets would turn to spattering mud, mixed with whatever trash and sewage had been left along them. A passing horse or wagon, or even a stumbling drunkard, would transfer this unsightly mixture to the outside of nearby houses. Rising damp, which found an easy traveling path through the porous coquina, left a series of jagged black stains from the ground up. Some degree of visual protection against these continual hazards was obtained by painting a dark stripe along the lower portion of the whitewashed walls. This was known as a *zocalo*, and some can be seen today.

54 St. George Street
Zocalo.

The parapets of flat-roofed buildings were pierced with spouts to drain off rainwater. These were called *canales*.

Another distinctive colonial feature is a gable roof with a raised parapet at the ends.

Once the buildings grew to two stories, balconies sprouted from them— to the extent that we find frequent complaints from visitors in the horseback age that the combination of narrow streets and projecting balconies made it hazardous to the head to navigate the thoroughfares. Exposed to the elements as they were, no original balconies survive on colonial buildings, though research has shown that some had simple supports while others featured more elaborate corbeling. Both types can be seen in their reconstructed forms.

Small dormer.

Wall dormer.

Some balconies have acquired Early American and Victorian details as well, showing the remodeling of this basic colonial feature over the generations.

Dormer windows found on houses also exhibit a variety of styles and changes over the years. The wall dormer is a colonial original. Shed dormers of an almost diminutive size also appear to be of early origin. It is necessary to remember that the roof is one of the most regularly replaced items on a building; its surfacing, underpinnings, and superstructure are all liable to have been modernized over the years.

Within the compound enclosed by the walls would be spaces for animals, a kitchen garden, and a well, which, as it played out, would be filled up with trash

Corbeled balcony support.

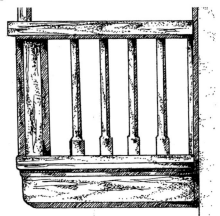

Plain balcony support.

267 CHARLOTTE STREET
One of the canales on a reconstructed house.

and left for future archaeologists, who would try to decipher the details of colonial life from its leftover garbage.

An open porch or *loggia* was a notable feature. Some were simple in construction and plain in detail, while others sported rather elaborately detailed masonry arches.

No colonial house has remained unchanged over the years, but all of the above details combine, in one building or in several, to give the distinctive St. Augustine look that has proved to be so marketable for the Ancient City in modern times.

42 SPANISH STREET
Gable roof with parapet ends.

CHAPTER TWO
The Early American Years

67 MARINE STREET

Early American buildings are quite rare in the Ancient City. This small house at 67 Marine Street, built before the Civil War, bears some similarities to its surviving contemporaries at 76 Spanish Street, 42 Bridge Street, and 28 St. Francis Street. It rests on a foundation of coquina piers, indicative of early construction. Over the years it has been owned by two St. Augustine mayors, W.S.M. Pinkham and W. W. Dewhurst. Notice how the siding on the dormer runs parallel to the roofline rather than to the ground.

PEOPLE WHO MOVE BRING THEIR ideas, for better or worse, with them. In Florida, so heavily populated over the years by outsiders, this is a cliché of utter exactitude. "Let me tell you how we did it back in New Jersey. . ." has become the stopping point of many a conversation.

The numbers were different but the sentiment the same back in 1821 when Florida belatedly became part of the United States. Andrew Jackson had done his damndest in the preceding decade to speed up the process by unauthorized invasions, as had a group known as "Patriots," who, at the time of the War of 1812, had sought to bring Florida under American rule.

Neighboring Georgians had complained long and loud and with violence that their slaves could slip off to Spanish or Indian sanctuary just across their southern border. The stirrings of Manifest Destiny demanded that the unannexed area to the south be acquired before turning full attention to the West.

Nor was the Spanish Empire having the best time of it—buffeted by the Napoleonic wars (even having a Bonaparte as king for a while) and facing rebellions and demands for independence from its American colonies. It finally decided to give up, and in 1819 signed the Adams-Onis Treaty which led in 1821 to the American flag being raised and the Spanish banner descending at St. Augustine's ancient Castillo de San Marcos.

This was followed by a new influx of public officials and the usual rush of fortune hunters. Those who poured into the new frontier often left a reputation none too savory behind. A Catholic bishop remarked with disgust that the old Spanish town was "overrun with Methodists and Presbyterians." The compliment was returned by a Methodist missionary who jotted in his diary that "the Catholicks are certainly the most profoundly ignorant people in this continent."

And what face did the Ancient City present to these newcomers? Not a prepossessing one: "it appeared ruinous, dirty and forbidding," according to an 1821 description. Another described its Second Spanish Period trajectory as "for years, declining in importance, and finally sunk into neglect and almost ruin."

What better circumstances for encouraging the presentation of bright new ideas? They were quick to appear.

"An extensive wharf, stretching before the town, should be immediately built—an Academy and Town Hall erected—a public walk planted, for the recreation of the inhabitants and strangers who pass the summer months here," wrote one go-getter who used the pen name "Americanus."

A committee of newcomers added its suggestion: "The old Convent or even the one half thereof would form an elegant and spacious College, and situated on the most airy spot of this Montpelier of North America would draw students from all parts of the Southern Section of the union."

There were other ambitious proposals as well, but the one that first turned out to be necessary was a Public Burying Ground, for hard on the heels of the change of flags came a yellow fever epidemic, which left dead in its wake the judge, the newspaper publisher, the Indian agent, the army surgeon, the president of the board of health, the district attorney, a city councilman, and others of less exalted position. As many were Protestants, they were not candidates for burial in the existing Catholic cemetery, and it was inconvenient to cart the corpses over to Fish Island where their co-denominationalists had previously been interred. The new cemetery was established right outside the city gates; perhaps a strange welcome for new arrivals, but one that continued through the twentieth century when the Visitors Center was moved into the building adjacent to it on the north.

If the newly American city developed fitfully and prosaically, rather than according to the greatest flights of fancy of its incoming boosters, still it was not without its attractions to observers in the coming years. It was a time when it was popularly said that St. Augustine made its living from "good oranges and sick Yankees"—the latter, of course, forming the basis for the modern Florida tourist industry.

A young and troubled New England minister who sojourned in 1827 in search of health wrote back home, "The air and sky of this ancient, fortified, dilapidated sand-bank of a town are really delicious."

He also noted some of its stresses and strains. Due to fear of Indians, he wrote, "All the old houses have very strong walls, and doors with apertures through which a musket can be discharged."

On a January day he "attended a meeting of the Bible Society. The treasurer of this institution is marshal of the district, and, by a somewhat unfortunate

94 SOUTH STREET, GARAGE

This building at 94 South Street may appear to be a garage, but it actually predates the automobile age by quite a bit. As I was checking out the age of buildings in this neighborhood, I noticed that the maps kept showing this structure, even before the houses around it were built. Closer examination showed it to be of sturdy coquina—not modern concrete block—construction. I called my friend X. L. Pellicer, octogenarian "King of the Minorcans," who had grown up across the street in the early years of the century. "That's the last slave cabin," he told me. It was part of Buena Esperanza plantation. Owners James and Hattie Lee White permitted an archaeological dig on the site for Black History Month in 1995 to see what information could be uncovered.

arrangement, had appointed a special meeting of the society and a slave-auction at the same time and place, one being in the Government House, and the other in the adjoining yard. One ear, therefore, heard the glad tidings of great joy, whilst the other was regaled with 'Going, gentlemen, going!' and almost without changing our position we might aid in sending the Scriptures into Africa or bidding on 'four children without the mother,' who had been kidnapped therefrom."

Despite these moral contradictions, he found his health improved. Penning a poem of gratitude, he took his leave and went on to write large his tripartite name in the history of American culture: Ralph Waldo Emerson.

The second decade of American St. Augustine was marked by the Seminole War, which broke out in 1835 when the Indians refused to be ever further removed from their lands to satiate the greed of newcomers. Plantations that had grown up north, south, and west of the Ancient City were quickly abandoned, and urban real estate prices skyrocketed as planters and their families sought safety. Particularly in demand was proximity to the old Castillo, recently renamed Fort Marion to honor the Swamp Fox of the American Revolution, many of whose fellow South Carolinians now headed south to do battle.

The beginning of the end of that war came with the capture, under a flag of truce, of the Seminole leader Osceola, just south of St. Augustine in 1837. Because of the circumstances, one of the participating soldiers would describe it with regret, nearly sixty years later, as "not a capture, but a breach of confidence."

Early American Details

Buildings change as years go by, and these pictures show details on colonial buildings that reflect what happened to them in the Early American years.

A second story was added to 143 St. George Street, and access to its balcony was provided by a bottom window sash that goes up and two small doors beneath that swing open. A similar arrangement can be found at 46 St. George Street.

31 St. Francis Street has an X-pattern balustrade on its balcony. This is one of the classic designs of the Early American period.

Many of the wooden buildings of that time used wider boards than were subsequently employed in St. Augustine. On 172 Avenida Menendez, the width of the boards on the left section, which dates from before the Civil War, can be compared with the narrower boards on the right from its Flagler-era addition.

143 ST. GEORGE STREET

31 ST. FRANCIS STREET

172 AVENIDA MENENDEZ

33 AVILES STREET

There are no pretensions to elegance in this Early American building at 33 Aviles Street, which is first mentioned in an 1844 deed to the property. Like the older colonial houses, it is built right near the street line. Any building that survives this long goes through a variety of uses. In 1888 and 1893, Sanborn Fire Insurance Maps list this as a "Negro tenement." In 1904 it was occupied by D. J. Trapps, upholsterer and mattress maker. In the 1920s it was the Benbow Inn (before such things were franchised). Later it housed the Fireside Artcrafters and Blue Gate Gift Shop. In the 1950s it was chopped up into efficiency apartments. In the 1980s it was returned to a single-family home, and a bizarre coat of stucco that had long disfigured it was removed to reveal the original boards beneath.

102 KING STREET

The cornerstone for 102 King Street was laid in October 1839 by the newly wed Dr. Andrew Anderson, Sr., and his wife Clarissa, who named the place Markland Hall after her brother Mark. Less than a month later, the doctor died of yellow fever, and it was left to his widow to supervise the completion (which took until 1842, even though the planned dimensions had immediately been reduced by half upon her husband's death). The finished product, with exposed coquina walls protected by wraparound porches, was described as "a typical southern home, with broad verandas over which a perfect wilderness of roses, honeysuckle and clematis grows." It was surrounded by one of Florida's pioneer orange groves.

Andrew Anderson, Jr., was born the year his father died and Markland Hall was launched. He also became a doctor. He served as mayor of St. Augustine and was the closest local friend of Henry Flagler. After his own marriage and the birth of two children, Anderson launched a major expansion that brought the house to its present configuration. He called on the services of a talented architect, Charles A. Gifford (1861–1937), who had previously designed the New Jersey Building at the 1892–93 Columbian World's Fair in Chicago. Flagler must have appreciated the remodeling work, because he recommended Gifford as architect for the Mount Washington Hotel at Bretton Woods, New Hampshire—famed as the place where the international monetary system was established at the end of World War II.

The Anderson family moved back into the new and enlarged Markland in 1901. In the years before his death in 1924, the doctor donated many public works of art, including the lion statues at the Bridge of Lions, for the beautification of St. Augustine.

Markland was sold in 1939 to H. E. Wolfe, a wealthy and politically powerful road builder and contractor. Senator Claude Pepper was a guest here in 1944. In 1968 Markland was purchased by Flagler College, which used it as a president's house for a time, and then as offices and classrooms.

Dr. Frederick Weedon, a physician and former mayor of St. Augustine, was present at the death of Osceola not long after in South Carolina. He removed the head of the Seminole leader, brought it back to St. Augustine with him, and hung it on his children's bedstead at night when they misbehaved.

The Ancient City had, through the centuries, learned the benefits of military subsidies. These became particularly essential to the economy in the late 1830s when agriculture was disrupted not only by the threat of warfare but also by the great freeze of 1835 and the subsequent invasion of the scale insect, which devastated the orange crop for decades to come. This was followed by the collapse of the mulberry mania which had had people all over the country spin-

ning silken dreams of great wealth, with Florida profiting as the nation's natural greenhouse.

Topping it off was the national financial panic of 1837 and subsequent economic hard times, which saw the collapse of many ambitious development schemes in St. Augustine as elsewhere.

Nevertheless, Florida survived, and in 1845, after an acrimonious internal debate, it became a state. This enabled it to fully participate in the acrimonious national debates centering on slavery, in a partisan fashion which modern Florida would probably rather not remember.

There was a tightening-up on the condition of blacks at home. Mayor George Fairbanks, a transplanted New Yorker now remembered as a pioneer

9 MARTIN LUTHER KING AVENUE

The Foster House at 9 Martin Luther King Avenue is one of the two surviving examples of Carpenter Gothic–style architecture in St. Augustine. Godfrey and Catherine Foster bought land in 1852 and built this house facing King Street. It was surrounded by a six-acre grove of 400 orange trees, along with figs, grapes, and roses. In the early 20th century this house was moved south to its current location, and a new house was built on its original site in 1914. The new house didn't fare so well; it was later demolished for the construction of a post office. One of the last family members to grow up in the old Gothic homestead was Andrew P. Foster, who went to West Point and became a general.

Florida historian, hailed "that wholesome relation of dependence of master and slave which is better for the servant & requisite to the master's proper control." This attitude was reflected in a whole raft of municipal ordinances.

One of the most visible public improvements of the Early American years was the building of a sea wall on the bayfront, which not only offered protection from erosion and flooding but also became a popular place of promenade. By 1852 a law was passed, saying: "it shall not hereafter be lawful for colored persons (bond or free) to use the sea wall as a place for promenading and they are hereby strictly forbidden to walk thereon, under a penalty of a fine of not less than two nor more than five Dollars, or in lieu thereof a number of stripes, of not less than ten nor more than thirty one, to be laid on the bare back of the offender."

The hospitality required for the nascent, but growing, tourist industry was increasingly replaced by hostility. After John Brown led his unsuccessful raid on Harpers Ferry in 1859 to free the slaves, the St. Augustine *Examiner* ran this warning under the bold headline "CAUTION":

"At the present time there are many persons from the North in the country who are in pursuit of health or pleasure. In the present excitable state of the public mind produced by the exposures of the Harper's Ferry plot, it is but natural that a feeling of anxiety and distrust should prevail. We trust that whatever opinions may be entertained by strangers unaccustomed to our institutions, they will have the prudence to keep their views to themselves, and we hope that our own people will act with judicious caution and not do injustice to the innocent."

St. Augustinian Buckingham Smith (1810–1871), a scholar and diplomat who used his postings in Spain and Mexico to dig up Florida's colonial records (thus becoming the ancestor of all the state's modern historians), favored preserving the union. But the majority of those who counted (as the city charter put it: "the free white male inhabitants") felt differently, and in 1861 Florida joined other southern states in seceding from the union.

Thus, within four decades, this pendant southern part of North America had been a Spanish colony, an American territory, a state of the United States, and part of the rebel Confederacy.

CHAPTER THREE
The Victorian Age

56 SPRING STREET

The house with these impressive curving Victorian porch brackets is located at 56 Spring Street in Ravenswood, an area that was developed after the Civil War with large lots for orange groves. The owner offered property for sale to Northerners only, thinking Southerners to be a rather slovenly lot. For three quarters of a century, 56 Spring Street was home to two generations of the Van family. John Van worked for the Florida East Coast Railway. His wife Mattie and their daughter Johnnie Mae Van were both schoolteachers with many decades of service.

ST. AUGUSTINE'S CONFEDERATE history was brief, if spirited. By 1862, Robert E. Lee (no stranger to the area, since he had charted the Ancient City's coastline a few years earlier as an Army engineer) decided that the small force at St. Augustine "serves only as an invitation to attack."

The portside location which had led to the city's settlement in the first place made it vulnerable to the maritime superiority of the Union navy, and after a hasty evacuation by Confederate troops and many of their local civilian sympathizers, a white flag was raised over the old fort and St. Augustine became one of several coastal Florida cities under Union control for the duration.

A succession of regiments from New Hampshire, Connecticut, Massachusetts, and New York headquartered in the city, and though they faced occasional sniping and some incivilities, it was generally considered a prize assignment, compared to the other possibilities. The historian of the Seventh New Hampshire Volunteers wrote affectionately several decades later: "We regretted exceedingly to leave St. Augustine, for we had found its climate very agreeable, and our accommodations had been much better than could be furnished to troops in garrison, even in time of peace."

And in tribute to its role as a rest and recreation center rather than a battlefront, he wrote: "The health of the regiment had steadily improved under the beneficent effects of the salubrious climate, and every man of our regiment will ever hold in the most pleasant remembrance the many happy hours passed at old St. Augustine, Fla."

"War is hell," indeed!

The revolving crew of soldiers included at least a couple who might be considered paragons of the two souls of Victorianism.

On the one hand there was Anthony Comstock, then a lad fresh from a Connecticut farm, just 19 when he enlisted to replace an older brother mortally wounded at the battle of Gettysburg. He stood out among his fellow soldiers by using his tobacco ration not for smoking but for making insect-repelling smudge pots. And rather than share whiskey, which he shunned, with his thirstier companions, he ostentatiously poured his ration of it out on the ground. He was given charge of Trinity Episcopal Church on the Plaza, and once again courted disfavor when he declined to open it "to the soldiers to use every night for singing

and pleasure," vowing in his diary to "keep sacred His house from everything that would pollute it."

He continued to act on these ideas in later years, becoming one of the nation's most famous crusaders. As an adoring authorized biography noted: "During the thirty years in which Mr. Comstock has been working for the suppression of vice he has destroyed over 43 tons of vile books, 28,425 pounds of stereotype plates, two and a half million obscene pictures and 12,945 negatives."

He also inspired George Bernard Shaw to coin the word "Comstockery," defined in Funk & Wagnalls dictionary as "Exaggerated censorship of literature, pictures, etc., because of alleged immorality."

If Comstock may be taken as a representative figure of the prudery for which Victorianism came to be remembered, one of his predecessor Union soldiers in St. Augustine became an exemplar of the reform strain which also flourished in that era, with effects still being felt in our own times.

Francis Wayland Parker came to the Ancient City with the first wave of soldiers, the Fourth New Hampshire Volunteers. Though he would eventually rise to command and colonelcy, being hailed as a war hero, his stint in St. Augustine was not the high point of his military career. He spent most of his months here under arrest and awaiting court martial on charges of drunkenness and "abusing his men by striking and choking them."

Whatever demons drove him, he presumably brought them under control as he went on to a distinguished career, not as a soldier but as an educator. He is often hailed as "the father of progressive education."

His own formal schooling was sparse. When asked the most important parts of his education, he cited five years on the farm and four years in the army. "In fact," he once said, "all through the army I thought a great deal of what I would do in school, and planned how I would change things." Whether his months of confinement in the Oldest City were particularly fruitful to that thought are, unfortunately, not recorded.

But his influence was such that his friend John Dewey ranked Parker and Horace Mann as the two most important figures in the history of American public education. A modern biographer has called him "The Children's Crusader."

St. Augustine has the distinction of being one of the few places where Abraham Lincoln's Emancipation

Towers and Turrets

The projecting tops of towers and turrets in various shapes—octagons, pyramids, cones, and mansards—add a delightful variety to the skyline of St. Augustine.

The Victorian age was a time when cigars were in vogue. Contemporary publications praised towers as an excellent place to which smelly smokers could be banished. Towers were also, of course, the capping decoration to the ultimate Victorian confection, the Queen Anne style.

That well-known Victorian, Dr. Sigmund Freud of Vienna, is remembered for his widely publicized theory about the symbolic significance of towers.

23 WATER STREET

99 KELLEY LANE

91½ KING STREET

The threatened demolition of the X. Lopez House for a post office parking lot in 1979 led to the formation of the Friends of St. Augustine Architecture, and thus it will always be remembered as the place where the tide began to turn against the wanton destruction of historic buildings in the nation's oldest city. The 1903 Queen Anne–style building with its tower and graceful curving porch was not torn down, but moved to 91½ King Street and turned half-way around. Unfortunately, bulldozers did in another building on the property, the former winter cottage of Dr. John Harvey Kellogg (1852–1943), inventor of breakfast cereal and peanut butter and leading character in the novel and movie *The Road to Wellville*.

59 CUNA STREET

11 BRIDGE STREET

139 ONEIDA STREET

80 SOUTH STREET

119 KINGSFERRY WAY—SHOTGUN STYLE

The shotgun style house, thin and long, running three rooms back from the street, is a Southern vernacular classic. Large numbers of them are found in New Orleans, Birmingham, and elsewhere. St. Augustine has its examples as well, like this gingerbread-trimmed house at 119 Kingsferry Way, though we lack the extensive neighborhoods of them that mark mill and mining towns where they provided the basic workers' housing. Recent studies have traced the origin of the style through free black carpenters back via Haiti to Africa, and consider it one of the cultural transferences from that continent to this.

Proclamation of 1863 actually freed the slaves. That document was carefully worded generally to apply only to areas under Confederate control, where it would have no legal effect. But this part of Florida was under Union control, and thus the slaves were gathered in a vacant lot on St. George Street (the site, between 234 and 244 St. George Street, is now known as Liberation Lot) and told of their freedom.

Some ex-slaves leased land from the city for one dollar a year on the west bank of Maria Sanchez Creek. They established a community first called Africa and then, as it expanded and streets were laid out, Lincolnville. The area grew to contain St. Augustine's greatest concentration of Victorian houses and was added to the National Register of Historic Places in 1991.

One unheralded event of the Union occupation was to have a great effect on the Ancient City's future history and development. That was the appearance in 1862 of a man with a camera: Sam A. Cooley, an official photographer for the U.S. Army's Department of the South. He became the first person to take extensive pictures of buildings around town, thus laying down the footprints in which many others would follow. A century later this early work would be essential in the restoration of historic buildings. The click of Sam Cooley's camera thus resulted in cultural and economic benefits for generations of people he never knew.

By the time the Civil War ended in 1865 (with St. Augustine native Edmund Kirby Smith as the last major Confederate general to surrender), the Ancient City was already launched into Reconstruction. Its slaves were freed, a school established, and all that was needed was to resuscitate the economy.

A variety of outsiders came to the rescue. Some were demobilized soldiers—or younger sons of English families not favored in the line of inheritance—who were lured by the prospect of striking it rich by growing oranges (or "golden apples" as they were called, for both visual and financial reasons). So prominent were the British among this crowd that when Sir Arthur Conan Doyle penned his Sherlock Holmes tale "The Five Orange Pips," it quite naturally included mention of St. Augustine.

There had been various schemes during the Civil War and after to settle freed slaves in the vast reaches of rural Florida; General Sherman even set aside a thirty-mile swath of North Florida for this purpose. The various projects turned out in some ways like the Minorcan settlement at New Smyrna a century before, with the colonists making their way to the metropolis of St. Augustine. Thus were a number of African-American soldiers from South Carolina introduced to the Ancient City.

Greater in number, though less permanent in residence, were the tourists who began coming to Florida once the hostilities had ended. They were a more varied group than their pre-war predecessors, who had been distinguished mainly by their racking coughs and other illnesses and infirmities.

Some were so delighted with the charms of the place that they built homes in the latest mansard style and became "winter residents"—a category so numerous as to become a standard designation in the city directories. They came from Kentucky and Vermont and Pennsylvania and New York and Massachusetts and other far-off places. They interested themselves in civic improvements like the planting of trees, production of plays and musical performances, and creation of a yacht club, historical society, and public library. Some of these benefits proved evanescent; others continued to be felt long after the lifetimes of their initiators.

Constance Fenimore Woolson, a woman of letters and grandniece of James Fenimore Cooper, was a regular visitor during the 1870s and left pen pictures of the Ancient City during that time in her correspondence and fictions. Of the social life, she commented: "The grandees are arriving and we are beginning to breathe that tiresome atmosphere of gold dust and ancestors which has oppressed us for two long winters. I always feel like a fraud when I go sailing with, say, six or eight incomes of six figures and the like. And then the an-

cestors. 'Her mother was a so-and-so, you know,' and 'his grandfather was a Van something.' The only thing we have to fall back upon is Fenimore Cooper, our one little anchor out in the crowded harbour. They have it now that Mother was his 'only sister.' We let it go so!"

Two things were required in the quest to relieve these people of some of their money. They had to be able to get to the Ancient City, and they needed a place to stay once they arrived. Hence, transportation and hotels were important developmental concerns.

It was the age of the steamboat, and the usual visitors would take one up the St. Johns River and debark at tiny Tocoi where they would wait (as one visitor put it) "amidst the heat and flies and dogs of the dirty station house" to make connections with the St. Johns Railway.

There was not much modernity about this line. Harriet Beecher Stowe, who traveled it in 1872, noted:

232 ST. GEORGE STREET—CARPENTER GOTHIC STYLE

It is not difficult to see why 232 St. George Street has come to be called the Gingerbread House. Ornamental woodwork hangs from the roofline like icicles, and the picturesque effect is heightened by the balcony and the diamond-shaped window-panes. This is St. Augustine's classic example of the Carpenter Gothic style of architecture that ushered in the age of Queen Victoria and reflected the technological changes brought about by the jigsaw and by balloon-frame house construction.

The house was owned after the Civil War by J. D. Stanbury, an attorney and justice of the peace. He died prematurely in 1877, but his widow lived to be 100, keeping the house for another half century. When her daughter married the local Presbyterian minister, Henry M. Flagler—a communicant of that church—made his private railroad car available to take the newlyweds on their honeymoon.

After Mrs. Stanbury's death, the Gingerbread House was owned by the family of Robert Gibson, who made his fortune inventing essential parts for the radio age.

Photo courtesy of David Nolan

A Portfolio of Victorian Gingerbread

88 BRIDGE STREET

30 MARINE STREET

45 CORDOVA STREET

78 SPANISH STREET

89 BRIDGE STREET

172 AVENIDA MENENDEZ

41 SAN MARCO AVENUE

28 SARAGOSSA STREET

160 M. L. KING AVENUE

268 St. George Street

9 Carrera Street

32 Saragossa Street

163 Oneida Street

Lightkeeper's House

36 Grant Street

99 Kelley Lane

103 & 101 Marine Street

96 & 98 Bridge Street

232 St. George Street

11 Bridge Street

"The railroad across to St. Augustine is made of wooden rails; and the cars are drawn by horses."

She added, "Travelers have usually spoken of this road with execration for its slowness and roughness." She herself did not mind the two to four hours it took to traverse the fifteen miles to St. Augustine because one of her winter occupations was painting watercolors of the native flowers, and she appreciated the leisurely opportunity to peruse them en route. Hers, however, seemed to be a minority opinion.

The line was upgraded later with a steam engine, and in the 1880s a rival group of investors had tracks laid directly from Jacksonville to St. Augustine, thus making for easier access.

As soon as post-war prosperity made it possible, up went the hotels: large wooden ones constructed of the then-plentiful, now largely vanished, heart pine, a sapwood relatively unappealing to boring insects but beloved by the licking tongues of fire. The tale of this age in almost any Florida town is the story of the "great fire," and St. Augustine is no exception. The hotels housed the visitors, and then practically destroyed the town when they burned down.

Major construction projects in colonial days were the work of the royal engineers. Later building in the Ancient City was generally the work of anonymous carpenters and masons. The Victorian age saw the appearance, here as elsewhere, of architects. Some may

8 ARENTA STREET—SECOND EMPIRE STYLE

The popular style of the Gilded Age after the Civil War was called Second Empire or—because of the leadership in Washington—the General Grant style. Its main feature was the distinctive four-sided, double-pitched mansard roof. (In modern times the roof has come to be more closely associated with *New Yorker* cartoonist Charles Addams and the haunted houses he portrayed.) St. Augustine, like other places in the country, blossomed with mansard roofs. Then, one by one, they burned, or were torn down as no longer stylish, or had their rooflines remodeled to other less-exotic styles.

The last house in the Ancient City to retain its original mansard is at 8 Arenta Street. It was built in 1886 as a duplex rental property for Rev. C. C. McLean, who was the first pastor of Grace Methodist Church. He had the dubious distinction of having obtained, in 1884, the enabling act permitting the Florida Conference of the Methodist Episcopal Church to divide into two separate groups: one black and one white. It had been the last integrated conference in the South.

The house itself is better known in connection with its longtime 20th-century occupants, the eccentric Barbour family. They (or the stories told about them, and the things they left behind) inspired a later owner, June Moore Ferrell, to write a Gothic novel *The House* (1979) set in this building.

62 LIGHTHOUSE AVENUE—OCTAGON STYLE

A colorful Victorian phrenologist and amateur architect named Orson Squire Fowler (1809-1887) popularized the octagon style in his book *A Home For All*, which gained wide-enough circulation in the 1850s to encourage the construction of a visible scattering of these dwellings around the country. The author asserted that an octagon shape enclosed 20 percent more floor space than a square with the same length of wall. Clarence Darrow was one notable American who grew up in an octagon house.

St. Augustine's classic Octagon House at 62 Lighthouse Avenue is a late example of the style, having been built in 1886 as one of the first two private homes (the other was at 8 Lighthouse Avenue) in what was projected as the city of Anastasia and has become, over the years, the neighborhood of Lighthouse Park. This is one of Florida's pioneer beach cottages, and its picturesqueness has always attracted creative people. Author Mary Antin, who wrote the popular 1912 memoir *The Promised Land*, rented it for a season, and it was owned for many years by artist Norman MacLeish, a brother of Pulitzer Prize–winning poet Archibald MacLeish.

have considered them merely puffed-up builders—and some no doubt were—but they had the great fortune of launching themselves in an age that believed, decoratively speaking, "more is better." The resulting confections—or those that managed to survive a period in the middle of the twentieth century when they were considered the height of bad taste—will continue to delight the eyes of the twenty-first century just as they did those of the nineteenth.

Once the visitors were here, they had to be both entertained and separated from their money. Otherwise, what benefit would they bring to the local economy? A variety of methods were devised. They could, for a fee, witness Dr. John Vedder's alligators

34 St. Francis Street—Italianate Style

With its projecting bay and paired cornice brackets, 34 St. Francis Street is about as good an example as we have of the Victorian Italianate style. It was built in 1889 and reflects one of the many experiments then being carried on here with concrete construction. It is a wood frame building with a concrete block veneer—perhaps the worst possible combination given the damp local climate and the prevalence of termites. Other examples of this type of construction have been lost over the years, leaving this period piece with only a few counterparts.

It was one of ten houses on the estate of John L. Wilson (1813–1899), who made his money in the West Indies trade and served as U. S. consul in Haiti. He is remembered as a benefactor in the Ancient City, having presented the town clock in the cathedral tower, as well as the Free Public Library building at 12 Aviles Street (now the St. Augustine Historical Society library). He also served as president of the Colored Industrial School. Over the years, 34 St. Francis Street has been a house, an apartment, a gift shop, an antique shop, and a newspaper office. It is located approximately on the site of the earlier home of the legendary free black man Antonio Proctor, a noteworthy figure in Colonial and Early American Florida.

80 Water Street—Queen Anne Style

Queen Anne was the ultimate Victorian style, mixing a little of this and a lot of that and topping the whole thing with a tower. 80 Water Street is a fine local example, mixing brick walls, shingled dormers, turned wooden balusters, and dentil moldings with a projecting pavilion and multiple rooflines. It is the oldest surviving brick private residence in town.

The house was built by Boston contractor John B. Canfield for John T. Dismukes (1847–1925), a Confederate veteran from Quincy, Florida, who came to St. Augustine in 1885 and established the First National Bank. He built and endowed the Dismukes Clinic at 24 Orange Street, which became the target of civil rights protests in the 1960s because it provided free dental care for white children only.

Later occupants of 80 Water Street included Dr. J. N. Fogarty, chief surgeon for the Florida East Coast Railway and the only man to serve as mayor of both Key West and St. Augustine. A longtime owner was Judge George W. Jackson, who may be best remembered in history for having performed the 1927 marriage of novelist Zora Neale Hurston.

The O'Brien House at Moultrie

This grand Queen Anne–style house overlooking the Matanzas River at Moultrie Point, south of St. Augustine, is the second-oldest poured concrete building in the area, after Villa Zorayda.

In 1980, exterminators checking the building found a bottle with a note inside in one of the first-floor vents. It read:

"This house is now being built by Henry Stanton O'Brien for a winter home for his family. I am his oldest son, Lewis Ogden O'Brien, and was 12 years old last Friday which was the 15th of May, 1885. There is six of us in our family viz, Mama, Papa, Grandmother, my two brothers, aged 9 and 5 yrs., and myself and there is about 43 (odd) acres in our place. I write this so that perhaps 100 years or more from now people will know who had this house built."

No message in a bottle ever accomplished its mission more perfectly.

In the 1920s this was the winter residence of Captain John L. Young (1853-1938), a leading figure in Atlantic City, New Jersey, where he ran Young's Million Dollar Pier, the amusement center of the resort. He lived in a Venetian-style mansion in the middle of that pier and used as his address "Number 1, Atlantic Ocean."

In 1931 the O'Brien House changed hands again and became the Dixie Home for the Aged and Infirm Deaf. A fundraising brochure described the work of the man in charge:

"The Superintendent of the Home has many duties. He tends the garden, keeps the water pumps, water heater and house in repair; the lawn trimmed; sees that there is plenty of wood stored before winter sets in, and looks after the fires in the Home, keeps the Chairman of the Board of Trustees informed on all matters pertaining to the Home, keeps financial records, looks after the correspondence and office work. In short, he is on duty 24 hours a day, 365 days in the year." Busy man!

The Dixie Home lasted through the Depression decade, but the property eventually returned to private use.

As it passed its first century, the secrets of its birth having been yielded up by the bottle, it was remarkably unmodernized, retaining gaslight pipes, natural ventilation systems, and original hardware, plaster, doors, and mantles to the extent that it was a veritable antique within and without.

99 KELLEY LANE

Victorian House Colors

Victorian house colors were a riot—almost literally. And, in the way that public fickleness has of switching from one style to its opposite, the Victorian years were followed by an era of white-on-white. It is much more difficult to appreciate details when they are presented in tones that make them blend almost out of existence.

We have taken a picture of 25 St. Francis Street as it appeared in 1994, painted white, and colorized it to show how some of the fine points of its construction might be better highlighted.

This is an appropriate house to start with, because in the 1980s it was saved from demolition. A proposal had been made to tear it down and put an imitation Colonial-style building in its place. For the first time, the state stepped in and cast its vote for saving the real building. It was a historic moment for preservation in St. Augustine.

Victorian Cut Shingle Patterns

321 St. George Street

28 Saragossa Street

164 Gault Street

9 Saragossa Street

86 Duero Street

Cartoonist Thomas Nast (1840–1902) may be considered our greatest symbolist. In the years after the Civil War, he gave us the Republican elephant and the Democratic donkey (both based on Aesop's fables), as well as the renderings we currently know of Uncle Sam and Santa Claus. He also visited the Ancient City. The Jacksonville newspaper reported on February 2, 1884:

"Thomas Nast, the well-known caricaturist, who has immortalized himself in the pages of *Harper's Weekly,* having been to St. Augustine during the day, returned to this city in the afternoon, considerably exhausted by his day's tour and the warm weather.

"Mr. Nast expressed great pleasure in seeing the Ancient City, but regretted the vandalism which was, by degrees, removing the ancient landmarks for the purpose of building boarding houses, etc."

One of Nast's daughters later married John W. R. Crawford, whose father was general manager of the railroad that linked Jacksonville and St. Augustine. The Crawford family home still stands at 50 Carrera Street.

160 MARTIN LUTHER KING AVENUE

CIVIL RIGHTS HOUSE   After the 1954 Supreme Court decision in Brown v. Board of Education said that segregated schools were inherently unequal and had to go, Southern states responded by establishing a variety of official commissions to see what could be done to preserve segregation as long as possible. Florida's contribution to this was called the Fabisinski Committee, headed by Judge L. L. Fabisinski of Pensacola. The judge grew up in St. Augustine in this elegant, century-old Victorian house at 160 Martin Luther King Avenue, but that's only part of the story.

Half a century after Fabisinski left, this was the home of Dr. Robert Hayling, African-American dentist who led the civil rights demonstrations to bring about an end to the very segregation the judge had tried to preserve.

There is no other house in St. Augustine—maybe none anywhere—that so clearly brings together the opposite sides of that great conflict which helped to shape American history. It has naturally come to be known as the Civil Rights House.

and other wildlife, penned in an old compound of colonial buildings on the bayfront (despite complaints from the neighbors about the resulting stench). Or they could get in a horse carriage and go for a scenic drive out the Horn Road (today's Masters Drive) and visit Ponce de Leon Springs, the Ancient City's first (but not last) "Fountain of Youth," conveniently discovered by the era's leading entrepreneur of tourism, a former New Jersey mayor named John Whitney. Some even took an invigorating sip from the springs, though one visitor wrote, "I am certain the generality of persons would prefer old age to drinking its waters."

Hours could be whiled away listening to the military band, or promenading on the sea wall, or wandering through one of those great Victorian jumbles known as museums. An observer in the 1870s noted a scene that must have warmed the hearts of local merchants: "the ladies are shopping in the tiny box-like shops in the narrow streets. They buy rich stores of brilliant wings of flamingoes, or pink curlews (all the hues of the rainbow are found on the feathers of the Florida birds), or they fill their pockets with alligators' teeth, curiously carved, or send home coquina vases, or

box a young alligator, a foot long, in Spanish moss, and express him North to a timid friend."

It was a place not without charm, but its attractions weren't universally felt. One moneyed visitor of that time, bringing his sick wife for the benefit of her health, hated the place and couldn't get out fast enough. "The accommodation was very bad, and most of the visitors here were consumptives," he later recalled. "I didn't like it, and took the first train back to Jacksonville."

Had he never returned, the history of Florida would have been vastly different.

CHAPTER FOUR
The Flagler Era

174 AVENIDA MENENDEZ

The Brooks Villa at 174 Avenida Menendez was built in 1891 in the Moorish Revival style so popular in the Flagler era. It was named for its owners, bachelor brothers Charles and Tracy Brooks, who were, according to the local society journal, "handsome and popular with their companions, and looked upon with longing eyes by every girl visiting the city."

In 1924 the house was purchased by Senator Frederick M. Sackett of Kentucky, who later served as American ambassador to Germany when Adolf Hitler came to power. Mrs. Sackett was a niece of Abraham Lincoln's closest friend, Joshua Speed, and his brother James Speed, who served as attorney general in Lincoln's cabinet. One of the things that Senator Sackett did in Washington was to seek an appropriation to preserve the Lincoln farm in Kentucky.

IF THERE HADN'T BEEN A FRANKLIN W. Smith, then perhaps he would have to have been invented—if anyone had come along with sufficient imagination.

By trade a Boston hardware merchant; by inclination a reformer; and by passion, from boyhood on, an architect, Smith was the man who reintroduced Spanish building and design into Florida, the father of the state's fantasy architecture, and the bright lightbulb that went off in the head of a person with sufficient wealth to transform Smith's dreams into St. Augustine's new reality.

Smith had all his life enjoyed making replicas of famous buildings from around the world (a London newspaper would dub him "Reproduction Smith" for this highly visible hobby). He started, of course, on a small scale, with models and birdcages, but by the time he bought property in the Ancient City to erect a winter home, he was ready for something in livable size. His design was inspired by Spain's famous Alhambra palace. His building material, poured concrete, was something he learned about on his travels in Switzerland. As his Villa Zorayda (named for one of the characters in Washington Irving's *Tales of the Alhambra*) rose, layer by layer, in 1883, it was an instant attention-getter for both style and substance. It was completed in time to impress the same man who had fled the Ancient City the decade before, when he first, briefly, brought his ailing wife hither. The wife had since died, and he had remarried. It was a liver ailment that sent him back south to St. Augustine, at the insistence of his doctor.

He was prepared for the worst, but wound up pleasantly surprised. He did not find himself surrounded by consumptives on this visit, but rather by "that class of society one meets at the great watering places of Europe—men who go there to enjoy themselves and not for the benefit of their health."

He was impressed with the town's new hotel, the San Marco, fascinated by the uniqueness of Villa Zorayda, and captivated by the ideas of Franklin W. Smith.

"I liked the place and the climate, and it occurred to me very strongly that someone with sufficient means ought to provide accommodations for that class of people who are not sick, but who come here to enjoy the climate, have plenty of money, but could find no satisfactory way of spending it."

His name was Henry Morrison Flagler. As the partner of John D. Rockefeller in the Standard Oil Company, he had plenty of money. And he had just found a satisfactory way of spending it; one that would consume the remaining three decades of his life, affecting every place from the Georgia border south to Key West, and leaving some wags to suggest that the abbreviation "Fla." stood not for "Florida" but for "Flagler."

The changes brought about during the Flagler Era in St. Augustine read like a list of the underpinnings of a modern city—for better and worse. Poles for telephones and electricity sprouted on the streets. Beneath those streets pipes were laid for gas, drainage, and water supply. The surfaces of those streets (some of them, at least) were paved with brick, asphalt, or cypress blocks (which proved unreliable, as they would float away in a flood). A bridge connected downtown

STATUE OF HENRY FLAGLER
A reporter once asked John D. Rockefeller if he had conceived the idea of Standard Oil. "No, sir," replied the billionaire. "I wish I'd had the brains to think of it. It was Henry M. Flagler."

83 KING STREET—VILLA ZORAYDA

Moorish Revival Style

The Ancient City has the nation's most extensive collection of exotic buildings in the Moorish Revival style. It is significant as the first reintroduction of Hispanic architecture into the former Spanish colony of Florida. Godfather of the style was Franklin W. Smith, who first used it for his winter home, Villa Zorayda, at 83 King Street, in 1883. The villa's interior features extraordinary cast plaster and tile work. Others adopted the style, and several homes and commercial buildings followed.

Smith's use of poured concrete construction was also pioneering; the other major project using that method at the time was the base for the Statue of Liberty. Some Moorish buildings used a less-expensive veneer of thin concrete blocks over a wood frame.

Moorish features were also tacked on to other buildings, like the masonry horseshoe arches on the otherwise wooden Queen Anne-style Upham Cottage at 268 St. George Street.

Some of the owners were as interesting as the houses they inhabited. Horace Walker, whose home at 33 Old Mission Avenue was a small domestic version of the style with a nice surviving fence, spent ten years in Pennsylvania drilling oil wells before coming here in the Flagler era to drill artesian wells. Late in life he gave up the trade to open an alligator farm.

Hugh de Laussat Willoughby (1856–1939) had a winter home at 8 Avenida Menendez called La Caseta (Spanish for "the cottage"), which was destroyed in the 1895 fire. A native of Solitude, New York, he was something of a Victorian renaissance man. He won the first athletic cup in University of Pennsylvania history, organized the Rhode Island naval reserve, learned how to pedal and balance from the inventor of the bicycle, played the first game of golf in Florida, was a pioneer explorer of the Everglades (writing a book about it), held numerous patents in the early days of aviation, and received praise as an artist as well. Nowadays, his name is used to sell real estate in south Florida.

These exotic period pieces of the Flagler era have been used as backdrops for movies featuring such stars as Theda Bara, Rudolph Valentino, and Rob Lowe. They are some of the great architectural treasures of St. Augustine.

Photo courtesy of St. Augustine Historical Society

8 AVENIDA MENENDEZ

33 OLD MISSION AVENUE

206 ST. GEORGE STREET

33 OLD MISSION AVENUE

268 ST. GEORGE STREET

to Anastasia Island, just as a railroad bridge over the St. Johns River at Jacksonville finally made it possible to take a train directly from New York to St. Augustine. The town acquired a new city hall, and the county a new jail. (Flagler didn't like the old one—a rickety affair from which prisoners regularly escaped—since it was inconveniently located across the street from his new luxury hotel.)

There was extensive resculpting of the land. The northern reaches of Maria Sanchez Creek were filled in (partly, it is said, with the archaeological remnants of the old Fort Mose site, which Flagler acquired to provide fill dirt), and on it Flagler built the grand Ponce de Leon and Alcazar Hotels and the first of his churches, Grace Methodist. The church was distinctively designed, but it was not his denomination, and he criticized his builders when he thought they were using too-expensive material on it. "Country sand is good enough for them," he instructed.

Albert Goodwill Spalding himself, the legendary pitcher turned sporting goods entrepreneur, was called in to design a ballpark, and on it played one of the nation's pioneer black baseball teams, composed of hotel employees—the team that came to be known as the Cuban Giants.

Land along the San Sebastian River was filled in and a train station and warehouse and industrial districts were created.

"Bet you can't eat just one" might well have been Flagler's motto. He had started out with the—for him—modest plan to build a hotel and recreational facilities at a cost of $200,000. But he wound up re-creating the nation's oldest city, then going on down the coast, building additional railroad mileage, picking up generous land grants, establishing farming communities populated by Swedes, Danes, Finns, Japanese, and others, experimenting in crops they could grow, constructing new resorts, and expanding or creating cities all the way down to Miami.

Hardly pausing, he then launched his most expensive venture: linking the string of islands all the way to Key West with "the railroad that went to sea." It was known as "Flagler's Folly," and he barely lived to see its completion. Largely deaf, blind, and frail when he road the first train there in 1912, he died the next year at the age of 83.

Despite the massive changes he wrought, it is worth noting two things Flagler did from which his successors in the Ancient City might have learned, though unfortunately they did not.

One is that very seldom did he tear a building down. He acquired much property that he had different plans for, but despite the difficulty—mules and rolling logs were the state-of-the-art technology—he moved buildings to other locations. Even today there are many surviving buildings that were transferred like checkers on a board by Flagler more than a century ago. His successors, unfortunately, have been more enamored of the bulldozer and wrecking ball, and the Ancient City's heritage has suffered accordingly.

Because the St. Augustine that Flagler found was a small town, the amount of building he did could easily have overwhelmed it and visually made the Ancient City vanish. Flagler himself did not care much for history, but he got good advice from his architect, Thomas Hastings. "I wanted to retain the Spanish character of St. Augustine," Hastings later said, "and so designed the buildings in keeping with the architecture of the early houses here with their quaint over-hanging balconies."

Thus, the new development made a conscious effort to fit in with the old, and after a century of aging, it would be hard to say which adds more to the storybook atmosphere of the city.

Flagler even carried it so far as having the streets rechristened with Hispanicized names—a dubious contribution, since much of any town's history is incorporated in its street names, and a lot was lost in the process.

Not only the looks and landscape of the area, but also its tastes and pleasures changed as Flagler attempted to transform it into the "Newport of the South."

The earlier Victorians prized a pallid, almost translucent, complexion and did their water frolicking indoors at Capo's Bath House on the bayfront where they felt protected from both sharks and the rays of the sun. Flagler's time saw the pioneer development of beach areas. North Beach, South Beach, Lighthouse Park, and Summer Haven all date from that time—and Florida would never again be the same. His hotels even maintained a cottage at South Beach for the use of guests.

St. Augustine proved to be not Flagler's destination, but rather his launching place toward the rest of Florida (and beyond: he also owned hotels in the Bahamas, as well as a steamship line to make them accessible). His initial impulse to make the Ancient City the "Winter Newport" expanded to a dream of making Florida's east coast the "American Riviera."

But it was not just that his interests expanded: it is also true that he soured a bit on St. Augustine and saw greater prospects elsewhere.

Why the souring? There were a variety of reasons. It was perhaps a harbinger of future difficulties when the opening of his Ponce de Leon Hotel was sandwiched between the devastating fire that destroyed the Plaza area and a yellow fever epidemic that resulted in the area having to be quarantined. If it wasn't too hot, it was too cold: freezes in 1886 and a back-to-back pair in 1894–95 destroyed the orange groves in this northern part of Florida and made Flagler more receptive to the

siren songs of those further south who were trying to lure him there, such as his old Cleveland neighbor Mrs. Julia Tuttle, hailed latterly as the "Mother of Miami."

Other places offered a chance to start anew, taking into account what he had learned in trying to deal with the nation's oldest city. That was an appealing prospect. He wrote to one of his associates in disgust: "I have realized from the beginning that St. Augustine was a dull place, but it does seem as though twenty years would stir up some little measure of public spirit; enough to at least keep the only street we have to the Railroad in decent condition."

Finally, the personal tragedies of his life had become entwined with St. Augustine, which thus became a repository of unpleasant memories. His initial visit to the city had been with his first wife, who died. His

20 VALENCIA STREET

UNION GENERALS HOUSE   This St. Augustine landmark, narrowly saved from demolition in the 1980s, was built in 1889 by the great Flagler contractors McGuire and McDonald as a winter home for the manager of the Ponce de Leon Hotel, O. D. Seavey. It reproduces the distinctive red and gray coloration—though not the Spanish style—of the hotel. One guest in the early years was the manager's brother, George Seavey, an artist renowned for his flower paintings.

The unique twist of fate that gave the house its name began in 1899 when John McAllister Schofield took it as his winter residence. He had been a Union general in the Civil War and served afterwards as Secretary of War, Superintendent of West Point, and commanding general of the U.S. Army. He may be best remembered for having gone to Hawaii in 1872 and making the recommendation that Pearl Harbor become an American naval base. Schofield Barracks there was named in his honor. The society newspaper here reported in 1899 that the retired general was "spending his spare moments on a tricycle and enjoying it." Schofield died of a cerebral hemorrhage at 20 Valencia Street on March 4, 1906, at the age of 74 and was buried at Arlington National Cemetery.

A decade later, the house was taken over by yet another Union general, Martin D. Hardin. A protegé of Abraham Lincoln (who first met his wife in the Hardin family home) and an aide, before the war, to Robert E. Lee, General Hardin continued his military career despite losing an arm (St. Augustine also had a one-armed Confederate general, William Wing Loring.) After leaving the army, Hardin became a lawyer. He died at 20 Valencia Street on December 12, 1923, at the age of 85 and is buried in the National Cemetery on Marine Street in St. Augustine. The La Leche Chapel on the grounds of the Mission of Nombre de Dios is a memorial to General Hardin, donated by his widow. Irene Castle, the famous dancer credited with popularizing the tango and bobbed hair, was Mrs. Hardin's sister-in-law and was a guest at the Union Generals House in the 1920s.

32 SEVILLA STREET

INGRAHAM HOUSE   When Henry Flagler built his railroad, the state gave him a vast amount of land—thousands of acres for each mile of track laid. To develop that land he hired one of the most experienced men in the field: James E. Ingraham (1850–1924). In what has been called Florida's "Age of the Three Henrys," Ingraham worked for them all: Henry Sanford, Henry Plant, and Henry Flagler. He also led a famous expedition through the Everglades and served as mayor of St. Augustine. The Ingraham Building, named in his honor, is a Miami landmark designed by the same architects who designed The Breakers hotel in Palm Beach and the Waldorf-Astoria in New York. Ingraham's home at 32 Sevilla Street, built in 1894 adjacent to the Flagler mansion, Kirkside, is the Ancient City's finest surviving example of Colonial Revival architecture. It served, for many decades after Ingraham's death, as the Presbyterian Manse, and later as church offices.

daughter Jennie died en route to St. Augustine in 1889 (Flagler dedicated the magnificent Memorial Presbyterian Church to her), and his last legitimate child, son Harry, was terminally estranged from his father after managing the St. Augustine hotels for a season. Flagler's second wife, Alicia, with whom he honeymooned in the Ancient City, slipped into insanity and was institutionalized for the last three and a half decades of her life.

"Happily ever after" was not the conclusion of Flagler's personal story in St. Augustine. It was more like a Greek tragedy than a fairy tale.

It is for long-term results rather than personal happiness that Flagler will be remembered. In 1885, as construction work began on the first of his Florida hotels, he wrote to his contractors McGuire and McDonald; "I think it more likely I am spending an unnecessary amount of money in the foundation walls, but I comfort myself with the reflection that a hundred years hence it will be all the same to me, and the building the better because of my extravagance."

Looking around the Ancient City a hundred and more years hence, one can only conclude that his remarks were prophetic.

The Shingles

The Franco-American impressionist Felix de Crano was one of the artists who came to St. Augustine in the Flagler era and took studios in the skylit back section of the Ponce de Leon Hotel known as Artists Row. There they exhibited their works and sold them to the wealthy winter visitors. A century later, their paintings are quite in demand by collectors. Mrs. de Crano belonged to a famous Philadelphia family. Her aunt, Rebecca Gratz, a friend of Washington Irving, was the original model for the character Rebecca in Sir Walter Scott's novel *Ivanhoe.*

In 1897, after several seasons in St. Augustine, the de Cranos bought a lot across from the hotel and in 1898 built a large winter home at 44 Sevilla Street. Its name, The Shingles, reflected its style—one that had been popularized in Newport and other northern resorts.

Although Felix de Crano died in 1908, his widow kept his studio open for another quarter of a century. When she died in the 1930s, she left The Shingles to benefit a local hospital. Over the years it continued to serve as a reminder of both the elegant winter "cottages" and the cultural life of Flagler-era St. Augustine. By the last decade of the 20th century it had become the Ancient City's only surviving example of Shingle-style architecture.

44 SEVILLA STREET

Photo courtesy of St. Augustine Historical Society

FELIX DE CRANO

On August 25, 1994, over the protests of local preser-
vationists, the de Crano house was demolished by
Flagler College.

DE CRANO DEMOLITION

"I look forward to an America which will not be afraid of grace and beauty, which will protect the beauty of our natural environment, which will preserve the great old American houses and squares and parks of our national past, and which will build handsome and balanced cities for our future."

—*John Fitzgerald Kennedy*

268 St. George Street

UPHAM COTTAGE   One of the most interesting "winter cottages" of the Flagler era, at 268 St. George Street, was built in 1892–93 for Colonel John J. Upham (1837–1898). A veteran of the Battle of Gettysburg and the Plains Indian wars, Upham hailed from Milwaukee, where his father had been a pioneer mayor. The colonel's 1891 marriage was followed by the construction of this house according to a design he and his wife created. They added features to it year after year, and it wound up in a basic octagon shape with a plethora of Queen Anne ornamentation. Its amenities included a conservatory, ballroom, and roof garden. It even had a glass-roofed Moorish extension with horseshoe arches.

After Upham's death, his extensive collection of Native American artifacts was given to the Milwaukee Public Museum.

Henry James, the expatriate American novelist, whose sister-in-law was a friend of the Upham family, was a guest here in 1905.

Though turned into apartments in the 1950s, the Upham Cottage has been under caring ownership in recent years and is one of the most eye-catching of our old houses.

234 St. George Street

VILLA FLORA   Villa Flora at 234 St. George Street was built in 1898 as a winter residence for O. A. Weenolsen, a Baptist minister who was pastor of the City Temple in Minneapolis. It has a raised basement (rare in low-lying St. Augustine) of coquina rock and a main floor of yellow brick, as well as the most extensive collection of stained glass in any local residence (even though one of the double-entry doors has been reduced, after an accident, to clear glass). Its shape is somewhat similar to Franklin Smith's earlier Villa Zorayda.

In 1906 it was purchased by Alanson Wood, one of the inventors of the roller coaster. After his death, his widow ran it as a small hotel. In the 1920s and 1930s it became a restaurant. Novelist James Branch Cabell, author of *Jurgen* (1919) and a longtime winter resident of St. Augustine, was particularly fond of it. In 1940, Villa Flora was bought by the Sisters of St. Joseph, whose convent is across the street, and it has been used since as a kindergarten and residence.

Summer Haven

Not everything developed in the Flagler era placed a premium on opulence. Take, for instance, one of Florida's pioneer beach resorts, Summer Haven. Located 18 miles south of St. Augustine, and not connected by bridge until 1927, it was remote and rustic and billed as a place to go to enjoy camp life. Today it is treasured as one of the rare places where Florida is as Florida was.

"RACING THE STORM"

Inland Floridians—from Crescent City, Pomona, Palatka, Satsuma, Welaka, Federal Point, and elsewhere—purchased lots in Summer Haven in 1886. The press reported, "On every side can be heard the sound of the hammer accompanied by the brisk tones of the workmen," predicting "Summer Haven will be a leading seaside resort in the future."

How did the resorters occupy themselves? One of them wrote in 1887: "During our stay there we had our entire time taken up in bass fishing, sheepshead fishing, catching turtles, stone crabs, gathering clams and walking

"SEAWAY COTTAGE" 9169 OLD A1A

"THE HUT AND THE LODGE" 9177 AND 9179 OLD A1A

"Old Summer Haven" 9135 Old A1A

hermit named G. R. Morse who arrived in 1887. When he died 20 years later, it was reported, "For several years he lived on 50 cents a week and what toll he took from the sea. As the years passed he became more and more of a recluse. His hair whitened and his beard, white as his hair, lengthened until it swept his breast. He evidently was quite proud of the patriarchal beard as he delighted in plaiting it and tying it with ribbon. For eight years he never left his solitary strip of sand." He figures as a character in the novel *Sheepshead Point* (1946) by Mary Mellon McClung, which is based on her reminiscences of Summer Haven.

the beach for turtle eggs." Some of their activities would not meet with the approval of future generations. "Shooting porpoises is another amusement which can only be enjoyed at this point, where you can either shoot them with a rifle or plunge a harpoon into them. They come within three or four feet of your muzzle. I killed one two days before I left."

Those were the daytime occupations. "At night euchre parties, yarn spinning, and singing are indulged in, and often a boat race is gotten up."

Summer Haven acquired a "mayor" in those years, a

"The Hut" 9177 Old A1A

"Last View" 8955 Gene Johnson Road

"FOR SALE BY OWNER" 8931 A1A SOUTH

Photo courtesy of Jack Genung

GENE JOHNSON, 1929.

Her family, the Mellons of Pittsburgh, were prominent 20th-century residents of Summer Haven. The coquina gateposts on Mellon Court mark the entrance to the old family compound. The main building was once operated as the Cove Tavern and attracted writers such as John Dos Passos, Robert Frost, and Marjorie Kinnan Rawlings. Ilya Tolstoy, grandson of the Russian novelist, once lived in Summer Haven. He was one of the founders of Marineland, the nearby oceanarium. A kind of swashbuckling adventurer, he also served as President Roosevelt's personal emissary to the Dalai Lama of Tibet during World War II.

The most famous area landmark for many decades in the mid-20th century was Gene Johnson's place. He was a black oysterman who, from his rustic cabin on the Matanzas River, served up oysters, clam chowder, fried fish, and pilau. Johnson's oyster roasts became so popular that sometimes whole Greyhound buses would be used to bring people in for them. Marjorie Kinnan Rawlings wrote about him in *Cross Creek Cookery* (1942). Summer Haven's main cross street is named Gene Johnson Road in his honor.

His place, which extended out over the river, was abandoned after his death in the 1970s but continued to attract interested people familiar with his legend.

When Jeanie Fitzpatrick started to paint a picture of it in 1989, she was saddened to learn that it was soon to be demolished. She took photographs and had to use them to complete the painting, as the original had vanished by the time the last brushstrokes were applied. She salvaged some wood from Gene Johnson's place and used it to make a frame for the watercolor, which she entitled "Last View."

St. Augustine Record. Photo courtesy of St. Augustine Historical Society

KIRKSIDE SHORTLY BEFORE DEMOLITION IN 1950.

KIRKSIDE APARTMENTS, 55 RIBERIA STREET.

Kirkside Recycled

Henry Flagler's mansion, designed by architects Carrère and Hastings, was named Kirkside because it was "beside the church"—the Memorial Presbyterian Church where the Ullman worshipped and was ultimately buried. Builders McGuire and McDonald began work in July 1892 and completed it in March 1893. After that, the local society newspaper, *The Tatler,* gave its readers a word-tour of the place. One room was "suggestive of Versailles," and there was much oohing and aahing over the display of "rare fans belonging to distinguished persons" and Mrs. Flagler's pride and joy, "the finest collection known" of historical miniatures representing European royalty. Due note was paid to the silver faucets and marble floors, and the whole was pronounced "a thing of beauty and a joy for ever."

Forever proved not to be a very long time. Mrs. Flagler's interest in royalty gave way to the delusion that the Czar of Russia was madly in love with her and that they communicated by Ouija board. She was declared insane and institutionalized for the rest of her long life.

A later occupant, Flagler heiress Louise Wise Lewis Lewis Francis, once proclaimed by *Forbes* magazine the richest woman in America, died tragically at 41 after three failed marriages.

In the 1940s, Kirkside was leased to the University Foundation, a Christian school that offered night and correspondence courses as well as a master's degree in religion.

In 1950 it was announced that the $20,000 required to fix up the place would be an unjustified expenditure, and Kirkside was demolished.

But if the owners did not value it, the same could not be said of the people of St. Augustine, who purchased parts of the old mansion and recycled them. The fanlight windows on the porch of 311 St. George Street (former home of baseball player Bill Steinecke) are said to come from Kirkside. A staircase and black-and-white tile floor are built into 77 Dolphin Drive (former home of Norton Baskin, widower of Marjorie Kinnan Rawlings). A colonial house at 42 Spanish Street was being restored at the time, and some of the wood from Kirkside was used in it. The pergola from the garden wound up at 12 East Park Avenue, and the greenhouse was moved to 8154 San Jose Boulevard in Jacksonville. Most noticeable of all are the columns from the mansion, which were built into the Kirkside Apartments at 55 Riberia Street, located on a corner of the once-grand grounds of the Flagler estate.

KIRKSIDE PERGOLA AT 12 EAST PARK AVENUE.

CHAPTER FIVE
Early Twentieth Century

PALM ROW

Palm Row began in the summer of 1904 with the construction of five rental cottages by contractor S. Clarke Edminster for H. P. Ammidown. The local newspaper reported, "The dwellings will be artistic in appearance, and will be equipped with baths, hot and cold water, and all other modern conveniences." A dozen were originally planned, but only one more was constructed: a duplex on the north side that went up in 1906. All the cottages were painted white. A brick street, 20 feet wide and lined with a row of palm trees, was marked on the north by a green area and on the south by a series of houses that repeated, one after the other, Victorian architectural elements: jigsawn brackets and bargeboards, chamfered wood posts, balconets, corbeled brick chimneys, etched glass, and shuttered windows. It became a favorite postcard view of the Ancient City.

Among the notable residents was Miss Emma L. Grout (1846–1926) of 3 Palm Row, who in September 1920 became the first woman to register to vote in St. Augustine.

The buildings have seen a variety of uses over the years—mostly residential, but also schools, a law office, a beauty parlor, a Christian Science Reading Room, and a gambling den. There was great local controversy in 1979 when 2 Palm Row, having previously been defaced with shingles, was subjected to the ultimate indignity of being covered with aluminum siding.

HENRY FLAGLER STILL LIVED, BUT by the dawn of the new century St. Augustine had become a way station in the resort world: a stopping-off point for the fancy folks en route to more elegant destinations like Palm Beach.

There were still "winter residents" and "winter cottages," but not so many new ones. When the annual reports were made on construction projects, those that drew attention, both on paper and on the streets, were the homes not of outsiders, but of prosperous local merchants—many of whom had made their money selling to the Flagler enterprises over the preceding decades.

Symbolic, perhaps, of the changes were the zigs and zags in the development patterns of Flagler's own Model Land Company, which owned the land between his railroad and his hotels. Early buildings on it included winter cottages for the hotel manager and physician, homes for executives of the railroad and other Flagler businesses, and a couple of large Queen Anne-style "cottages" that were rented seasonally to hotel patrons who desired larger accommodations. Flagler was a man with fixed views about social status that were reflected in the size and design of these buildings. The residence of the housekeeper would not outshine that of the manager of the hotel, nor would the assistant passenger agent live more elegantly than the vice president of the railroad. Flagler, who had himself risen out of poverty, showed little inclination to mix with poor people in his later years. His contribution to Florida was not in the field of democratic theory or human rights; those things required other champions. But in brick and terra-cotta and poured concrete and stained glass and millions of board feet of lumber painted "Florida East Coast Yellow," he was truly a world beater.

Once Flagler decided to forsake St. Augustine for Palm Beach, the local developments of his Model Land Company diminished accordingly in grandeur. At the western end of the tract—less elegant because bordered by the railroad track—the block size was sliced in half to create smaller, more densely populated streets from which rose the popular twentieth- century bungalows, designed for sturdy employees but not those in high executive ranks.

Progress was its usual terrible self.

A row of moss-draped live oak trees ran down the center of King Street, providing shade and atmosphere to both lanes of the city's main east-west artery. They were there because when Henry Flagler had the street widened in the 1880s he declined to have them cut down, instead leaving them as a median with the second lane put in on their other side.

They stayed that way for two decades, until the streetcar lines appeared in the early 1900s. Then they were leveled to make way for the tracks.

The newspapers of the time were filled with regular reports that such-and-such dilapidated coquina building was being torn down so that a spanking new brick business block could be constructed. It was always announced, hosanna-like, as a great improvement to the community. Half a century later, many of those new business blocks would be demolished so that imitations of the old coquina buildings could be reconstructed, at great cost, as part of the restoration program

Photo courtesy of St. Augustine Historical Society

ALBERT SMITH'S FISH SCALE HOUSE

FOLK ART HOUSE "Everybody in town knows Albert Smith, a colored genius, who is perhaps alone as an architect who builds houses out of fish scales," reported the local paper in 1903. The occasion was the announcement that Smith's largest production, a two-story house that required nine barrels of drumfish scales to build, was scheduled to be exhibited at the St. Louis World's Fair of 1904. A banker from that city had seen it on his winter sojourn in St. Augustine and agreed to bring Smith, his family, and his creation to the fair, with backer and builder to split the admission fees half and half. The St. Augustine Historical Society has a much smaller work of Smith's called "Facsimile of the St. Augustine Cathedral."

Concrete Block Houses

St. Augustine had been an important place for experimentation with concrete construction in the late 19th century, as the landmark churches and hotels of the Flagler era show. By the early 20th century, the concrete work done in the Ancient City was on a more domestic scale. B. E. Pacetti made his own concrete block (called artificial stone) and used it to build several houses and walls around town. 17 Cincinnati Avenue, built about 1910 for Fred M. Allen, city editor of the *St. Augustine Evening Record,* may have been Pacetti's last before his premature death. It bears comparison with earlier Pacetti houses at 15 and 17 Old Mission Avenue.

24 Cincinnati Avenue is slightly later and represents the next step in the evolution of local concrete block construction. This block gets its golden coloration from a significant admixture of local coquina shell. The house was built in 1914 by Fred Capo, a blacksmith for the Florida East Coast Railway and member of a prominent Minorcan family. The press reported at the time, "Mr. Capo works after hours making stone blocks and has made every block in the residence." This was no small feat, as a variety of different patterns was used. It is a house that is worth a close look—and then yet another.

17 CINCINNATI AVENUE

24 CINCINNATI AVENUE

in the downtown area. Though the resulting appearance may have been similar, like a forged autograph or copied painting or counterfeit dollar, the imitation would never have the same value as the original.

The national symbol of all this progress was the president, Theodore Roosevelt, who visited the Ancient City in 1905. He was a man whom Henry Flagler truly loathed, for his trust-busting and other policies.

"I have no command of the English language that enables me to express my feelings regarding Mr. Roosevelt," wrote the Florida magnate. "He is shit."

Things that had been rare in Flagler's time now became more widespread or even commonplace: telephones, electricity, and, of course, automobiles. Everyone's grandfather seems to have had "the first car in St. Augustine." All those simultaneous pioneers must have created quite a traffic jam on the streets!

The two most famous national road-building projects of the time were the Lincoln Highway, which ran east-west, and the Dixie Highway, which ran north-south. St. Augustine's chunk of the Dixie Highway was proudly paved in brick, unlike other stretches where mud and potholes made it a memorable driving experience.

Ironically, the same automobile that conquered space and altered time and resulted, ultimately, in the paving of large parts of America, also created a desire for picturesque destinations. Who, after all, would take a long journey merely for the pleasure of seeing a gas station or parking lot no different from those at home? So, many old buildings from coast to coast were fixed up either as museums or antique stores or Tea Shoppes—the latter considered a respectable occupation for widows with more blue blood than greenback

Palm Tree Posts

The immediate inspiration for the use of native palm tree trunks as porch posts on houses came from Artists Row, the back section of the Ponce de Leon Hotel, one story above Valencia Street, where a whole string of them lined the way to the studios. The theme was picked up in nearby outbuildings like 8 Valencia Street, on the grounds of the Albert Lewis estate, and the Billiard House behind Dr. Andrew Anderson's mansion, Markland, at 102 King Street. In the Billiard House, the palm tree posts vie for picturesqueness with the concave, four-sided roof. Palm tree posts represent a Florida counterpart to the rustic Adirondack style so popular in northern resort architecture.

A second wind came with the bungalow style in the early 20th century, given its affinity for using natural native building materials. Fred A. Henderich, St. Augustine's premier bungalow architect, made liberal use of palm tree posts, most visibly on houses along a stretch of St. George Street south of St. Francis Street. Posts appeared on larger buildings as well. Miramar at 21 Water Street, overlooking the fort and bayfront, which Henderich designed in 1905 for General W.N.P. Darrow, originally had them, though they were replaced in a later remodeling. The A. B. Day House at 404 Old Quarry Road on Anastasia Island, built in 1917 by Goold T. Butler, features a whole three-sided arcade of paired posts.

Sadly, many houses have had their palm tree posts replaced with more prosaic materials. I once asked a local architect why this happened. "There's no stress rating in the Southern Building Code for palm tree posts," he replied.

404 OLD QUARRY ROAD

287 ST. GEORGE STREET

8 VALENCIA STREET

MARKLAND BILLIARD HOUSE

dollars. St. Augustine got its share of these, and the resulting cash flow helped to preserve some of the older buildings at a time when so many of their contemporaries were biting the dust.

It would have helped if George Washington had slept here—preferably in several different locations—but alas, he never seems to have made it this far south.

Not all new transportation forms were on the ground. Aviation also made its appearance. Just as the Wright Brothers used the beach at Kitty Hawk, so too did the sands of St. Augustine provide a place for takeoff and landing. In 1911, J.A.D. McCurdy, who had previously made the first flight in Canada, became the Ancient City's pioneer aviator in an exhibition that drew crowds, not all of whom, unfortunately for the promoter, paid for the privilege of watching.

When World War I broke out, Canadians came to St. Augustine's North Beach to learn how to fly. When America entered the war, the first man-made landing field was built on the grounds of the St. Augustine

298 St. George Street

In 1910, contractor Fred Walton built what was described as a "Spanish bungalow" at 298 St. George Street for a distinguished client: Simeon Baldwin (1840–1927), chief justice of the Connecticut Supreme Court who was, that same year, elected to the first of two terms as governor of the state. In 1912 Baldwin was a candidate for the presidential nomination at the Democratic National Convention, but lost out to his fellow governor, Woodrow Wilson. Baldwin served, at various times, as president of the American Bar Association, the American Historical Association, and the American Political Science Association. Indeed, one biographical directory noted that Baldwin "held far too many offices to list in full but all of them adding up to the undisputed title 'The First Citizen of Connecticut.'" He taught at Yale Law School for half a century and was associated with Yale Farms, an agricultural project in the Lincolnville section of St. Augustine.

His father, Roger Baldwin (1793–1863), was also governor of Connecticut but is best remembered as the defense lawyer for the slaves who mutinied and took over the ship called *Amistad* in 1839 and won their legal freedom with his assistance and that of former President John Quincy Adams, who successfully argued their landmark case before the U.S. Supreme Court.

In the 1920s, 298 St. George Street became the family home of Edith Taylor Pope (1905–1961), who made her mark as an author. Her 1944 novel *Colcorton* was a runner-up for the Pulitzer Prize.

177 Surfside Avenue

SINCLAIR LEWIS HOUSE The shingled bungalow at 177 Surfside Avenue in North Beach is significant to history as the place where Sinclair Lewis (1885–1951) launched his career as a full-time writer in the early months of 1916. In 1930 he became the first American to win the Nobel Prize for Literature.

After selling several stories to the *Saturday Evening Post* in 1915, Lewis quit his job writing promotional copy for a publisher and resolved to live by freelance writing. He came to St. Augustine and rented what his wife called "the littlest house with a veranda as wide as itself, supported by palm-trunks and looking toward St. Augustine across the bay." On a marble-topped desk in the bedroom he worked on a variety of projects. One was described by critic Mark Schorer as "almost certainly the worst thing that Lewis ever wrote," but another was hailed as "the first sustained work recognizably written by the author of *Main Street.*" Lewis returned to St. Augustine in later years and always remembered his first visit fondly.

For many years I kept an eye on the fate of this cottage, always worrying that its location on several waterfront lots would lead to its demolition. When it was sold and the new owners held a garage sale, I went to talk with them about the historic importance of the place. They were pleasantly interested, and the man of the house showed me around. As I left, I said "I know your last name, because it's on the mailbox, but what's your first name?"

"Sinclair," he replied and I stopped worrying, at least for the time being.

322 St. George Street

CLASSIC BUNGALOW   322 St. George Street, low-slung and horizontal, with overhanging eaves, open gablework, pergola, and battered porch posts is a classic of the bungalow style. It is part of a notable cluster of them located in the neighborhood surrounding Maria Sanchez Lake.

It was built about 1915 for the newly married son of the family that lived in the large Victorian house next door; the two houses together give a dramatic visual example of the change of architectural tastes from generation to generation. Residents have included Robert Meserve, who served as Superintendent of Schools; Herbert Felkel, editor of the St. Augustine Evening Record; and John B. Mulvey, real estate investor for whom Mulvey Street is named.

Country Club at the south end of Lincolnville. It was completed just as the armistice was signed, and so, apart from a crash landing, saw little official use.

Aviation figured in scenes shot here for the popular movie serial "The Perils of Pauline" starring Pearl White. Many silent films were made in St. Augustine in the early decades of the century, featuring stars such as Rudolph Valentino, Billie Burke, Ethel Barrymore, and Theda Bara. A promotional brochure sent to moviemakers touted local beaches as ideal not only for desert pictures, but also—given the fine white quality of the sand—for Arctic snow scenes as well.

Movies pumped a little money into the local economy (at least the filmmakers complained they were being overcharged for props and other materials by local entrepreneurs), but eventually Hollywood, on the other coast, became the favored location, and the exciting sound of "lights, camera, action" would be heard only at long intervals, not enough to register more than a blip on the scale of financial well-being.

More productive of regular payrolls was Flagler's Florida East Coast Railway, which had its headquarters and shops here.

The Spanish-American War of 1898, and the fear among coastal residents that they would somehow be attacked by a new Spanish Armada, had increased the military presence in town for defense as well as rest and recreation. In the aftermath, however, the fort and barracks were closed down as active military sites, though some of the slack was taken up when the state military headquarters was moved to the barracks and the fort became a popular tourist attraction.

The profile of the tourist was changing. Promotions in the early twentieth century stressed, "You don't have to be rich to come to St. Augustine." The calendar of the tourist season changed as well. In those pre-air-conditioned years, and with yellow fever under control, the ocean breezes made the area a summertime draw, just as the freezes of the 1890s had proven that winters could be something less than paradisiacal.

There was great excitement in 1911 when it was announced that Anastasia Island had been selected as the site for the Methodist Church's summer Chautauqua. It was one of more than a hundred locations nationwide that provided adult education, growing out of the movement begun in 1874 at Lake Chautauqua in upstate New York. Many areas had competed for the honor, but St. Augustine came up with the best offer: 200 oceanfront acres to be donated by the Model Land Company and $10,000 to be raised by the Board of Trade through public subscription. The area—which would be incorporated in 1959 as the city of St. Augustine Beach—was a pioneer summer resort here, and the local newspaper confidently predicted that "Anastasia from end to end will be settled with summer homes within a very few years." By the end of the century, at least, that remark had a deadly accuracy.

Modern residents might look back with humor on the initial assertion that "No saloons will ever be permitted about the grounds and there will be a Christian influence evident in the community. But there will be no lack of amusements, the main stipulation being that there will be no Sabbath desecration."

The design of Chautauqua Beach (as it was originally called) was an interesting one, with the main road punctuated by a series of plazas, like Savannah, Georgia. The basic plan remained, generations later, one of the best hidden assets of the town.

Areas inland from the beach also found new economic uses during the early twentieth century. Hastings, Elkton, and Spuds, with the help of drainage ditches, became the center of Irish potato growing.

The San Sebastian River, dividing St. Augustine from West Augustine, became the home in the 1920s of

63 BAY VIEW DRIVE

COLONIAL REVIVAL   The more starched burghers in the age of bungalow informality might opt instead for the contemporaneously popular architecture of the Colonial Revival, which became widespread after the nation's centennial celebration in 1876 and continued over the next half century. It gained added impetus as some looked with dismay on the rising tide of immigration that also marked the era.

Judge Robert F. Hopwood (1856–1940) of Uniontown, Pennsylvania, made his winter home in this Colonial Revival building at 63 Bay View Drive. An active Methodist Sunday School superintendent as well as an avid golfer, Hopwood had been elected in 1914 from his native state to the U.S. House of Representatives. While there he combined his religious and political views and —as was reported in a local interview—"he voted for every measure which would bring about temperance legislation, and in that way lost his opportunity to be returned to Congress, as he was defeated for a second term by the liquor interests in his congressional district."

shrimp boat fleets, moved down here from Fernandina. Italians were prominent in the shrimping industry, and one of the boats was proudly named *Benito Mussolini*—before the outbreak of World War II.

There was even an attempt to steal the cigar manufacturing business from Tampa. Cigars had long been made here, mostly by small producers working in lofts and outbuildings, though even city hall and the old convent shared space with cigar factories.

Between 1907 and 1909, the Board of Trade raised $13,000, sent an architect to Tampa to borrow the best designs from the factories there, and signed an agreement to give the new facility at 88 Riberia Street to the Solla-Carcaba firm if they could produce 8,000,000 cigars in five years. They went bankrupt instead. Their successors, Pamies & Arango, did succeed in fulfilling

Bungalow Combinations

The bungalow style freely mixed in hybrid fashion with other contemporary designs. Among the examples found in St. Augustine:

9 VENANCIO STREET—ORIENTAL

22 EAST PARK AVENUE—TUDOR

9 MILTON STREET—PRAIRIE

54 BAY VIEW DRIVE—COLONIAL

the terms of their 1920 agreement to manufacture 7,000,000 cigars within ten years, but their success came at a time when cigarette sales were surpassing those of cigars and the economy suffering real estate bust and stock market collapse. The bank took the building over in 1930—then it, too, went under. St. Augustine was not destined to steal Tampa's business.

The Ancient City received a shot in the arm in 1918 when the F. N. Holmes livestock farm on West King Street was taken over by an African-American school. Begun in Jacksonville in 1892 as the Florida Baptist Academy, it expanded here as the Florida Normal and Industrial Institute, then united with another school to become Florida Memorial College. From its opening ceremonies in October 1918 (Daytona educator Mary McLeod Bethune was one of the speakers), the institution provided valuable training and jobs. For half a century it would be a St. Augustine fixture.

But the early years of the twentieth century were difficult ones for African-Americans. A concentrated effort to turn back the gains in black political power after Reconstruction had resulted in a new constitution for the state in 1885 and a new city charter soon after. The number of black elected officials diminished, then ended, symbolically, on the 1902 day when the local newspaper reported, "Without a word of warning and with nothing on the surface to indicate the cause of his act, . . . Marshal Charles Benet drew a revolver at a meeting of the City Council last night and shot Alderman John Papino."

Benet was white; Papino black.

The account continued: "To say that the sudden onslaught of the infuriated marshal created a sensation would be putting it mildly. While Papino was dodging to escape the bullets, Alderman Center is said to have made record time to the door. He was followed by Alderman Pacetti, who suddenly remembered an important engagement at a union meeting. Clerk Carrera devoutly crossed himself and executed a rapid descent to the street. President-elect McBride remained perfectly still, not knowing whether or not the marshal would turn his batteries on him. He stayed there until someone asked him for a match, and then he, too, skedaddled."

Perhaps more shocking than the shooting was the fact that the marshal was never called to account for it. But in the long run there was some justice in that

Papino survived his wounds and long outlived Benet, who died at the age of 44 from kidney disease.

Other items could be ticked off from those dreadful decades: 1907 saw both the division of the railroad waiting room into "white" and "colored" sections, and the beginning of a white primary, to make it impossible for blacks to have a vote in selecting candidates for office. In 1910 it was made illegal to show movies of boxing matches—after black heavyweight champion Jack Johnson defeated James J. Jeffries, one in a series of Great White Hopes. In 1916, three of the Sisters of St. Joseph at St. Benedict School in Lincolnville were arrested for violating a law that forbade whites to teach blacks. Though they were eventually acquitted, there was nothing reassuring to the egalitarian when the judge upheld "the teaching of the Negro in Sunday Schools and day Schools by those best fitted for such work, the superior and educated white race," nor when he further noted: "To say that such teaching would have a tendency to promote social equality among the races and thus be opposed to the good morals of the State is to insult the superior race and ignore the relative status of teacher and pupil."

When a black physician purchased a previously white-owned house, he was forced to announce publicly that he would rent it only to whites, although blacks lived all around the neighborhood, and he himself lived right next door.

Editorials in the local newspaper called for laws against integration, saying: "Instances have occurred in this city wherein white people have vented their spite on a next door neighbor by selling their own homes to negroes, but a segregation ordinance would have prevented this." It touted the justice of this, claiming "no injury would be imposed on negro residents if they are confined to a certain section of the city, but a decided injury is inflicted on the white property owners if their homes are not protected."

When the Ku Klux Klan held its first parade in St. Augustine in 1922, it made sure to march through Lincolnville, hoping to spread a little terror.

The discriminatory aspects of segregation demonstrated a mean streak running through the soul of the community. They also led to the creation of a number of black businesses. A leaflet put out in the 1920s by the Colored Business and Professional Men's League urged people to patronize their own, and included a long list of barbers, cafes, gas stations, dry cleaners, drug stores, grocers, insurance agents, doctors, shoe repairers and undertakers, mostly on Washington Street, which was the main business district of Lincolnville.

The Ancient City's looks changed considerably in the early years of the twentieth century.

Many landmarks that had not been torn down burned down in the terrible 1914 fire that rivaled that of 1887 in its destructiveness. A whole stretch of colonial buildings along Charlotte Street that had been a favorite among both artists and postcard photographers was reduced to rubble. (The loss was not total: moviemakers used the resulting scenes to depict war-ravaged Europe. It was a safer place for them to shoot—one where they would not be shot at in turn.)

In the aftermath of the fire, wood shingle roofs were outlawed. The shingles had shown a disconcerting tendency to burn loose at the narrow end, then fly like flaming frisbees onto neighboring roofs to spread the inferno. No new ones were to be applied, and those already in service were to be replaced within a decade.

The twentieth century brought that trinity of municipal improvements to the nation's oldest city: the city manager form of government, zoning, and planning. Looking back today on some of the early plans for improvements is a stitch indeed: they were so obviously the visionary attempts of politicians and businessmen who dwelt in an everlasting now.

Different types of land use came with the new century. In 1904 Palm Row was created: a brick walk running between St. George and Cordova Streets, lined with parallel rows of palm trees. The houses along it were perpendicular rather than parallel to the main streets at either end.

A few years later, St. Andrews Court was cut through off Cordova Street, and Marwin Terrace off nearby Carrera Street. These were St. Augustine's counterparts to California's plentiful bungalow courts.

Then came the development of the west bank of Maria Sanchez Lake in the 1920s. The houses were built facing the lake, separated only by a sidewalk. The road was behind them. It is interesting to look from there to the older neighborhood across the lake, where houses back up to the water and are separated from it by a street: in earlier days the lake was a place to dispose of garbage, not something you wanted to watch from your front porch. Thus did different generations approach their natural assets in different ways.

Land use was only one way in which the new century differed from the old. Victorian verticality and frilliness gave way to Edwardian stolidity and boxiness. That, in turn, gave way to bungalow informality. These changes in architectural style matched others in clothing, manners, and general design. Queen Victoria and Henry Flagler might have been horrified, but their descendants found them all a vast improvement.

CHAPTER SIX

The Boom

107 OGLETHORPE BOULEVARD

Plans for the development of Davis Shores during the 1920s boom were grandiose, but the number of buildings actually completed was quite modest. The largest of the houses, at 107 Oglethorpe Boulevard, was intended for Robert R. Milam, the general manager of Davis Shores. He was a Jacksonville attorney with fruit and fertilizer interests, and younger brother of Arthur Y. Milam, the speaker of the Florida House of Representatives and vice president and treasurer of D. P. Davis Properties. Unfortunately, the house was not ready for occupancy when financial difficulties and the 1926 hurricane knocked the props from beneath the boom.

IN THE AFTERMATH OF WORLD WAR I, people couldn't wait to live it up. In the 1920 presidential election, victory went to Senator Warren G. Harding of Ohio, who promised "a return to normalcy." In the weeks before his inauguration, he sojourned—as he had before—in St. Augustine at the Ponce de Leon Hotel. There he selected what came to be known (at least until Watergate) as the most corrupt cabinet in American history. He also sampled the golf links, tried his hand at fishing, and helped to focus national attention—that year and the next—on what was to be one of the great phenomena of the decade: the rediscovery, with a vengeance, of Florida.

Booms were not a new thing to the Sunshine State. One occurred after it became part of the United States in 1821, another followed the Civil War, and a third began with the coming of Henry Flagler. But the boom of the 1920s was the one that came to define the term, then and forever. Its zaniness was such that the Marx

16 MAY STREET

THE PINK CASTLE The Pink Castle at 16 May Street was built in the early 1920s as home and studio for C. Adrian Pillars (1870–1937), the most famous sculptor to live in the Ancient City. He honed his skill from the age of 12, working for and studying with Lorado Taft and Daniel Chester French. Each state is able to immortalize two of its citizens with statues in the Capitol building in Washington. Florida chose Dr. John Gorrie, inventor of the ice machine (seen as predecessor to the air conditioner), and Confederate General Edmund Kirby Smith (a native of St. Augustine). Pillars sculpted both statues. For the Ancient City he designed the World War I memorial flagpole in Anderson Circle on the bayfront. In Jacksonville's Riverside Park, Pillars' monumental statue of Winged Victory (for which two St. Augustine youths modeled) is one of that city's artistic treasures. In 1932 he moved to Sarasota to teach at the Ringling School of Art. The prominent location of Pillars' Pink Castle on Highway A1A leading into the city makes it one of our most visible landmarks.

Brothers' movie version of it, *The Cocoanuts*, seems tame by comparison. Of course, when it first came on the scene it was treated solemnly and seriously. After all, there was money involved—though most of it was on paper; not yet cash, but promises to pay cash at some time in the future. The future, however, had different plans.

It was a product of the times. The Roaring Twenties were the age of bootleg whiskey and bathtub gin, of jazz and flappers, of modern art and lost generations, of the Ku Klux Klan and William Jennings Bryan.

This Bryan, in his final incarnation, was no longer the Boy Orator of the Platte railing against the Cross of Gold, but rather a political evangelist and seller of Florida real estate, based in Miami.

The real estate he sold came on curving streets lined with tropical foliage and white-way lighting. The houses were stucco and had red tile roofs. The lots bordered on water: either the real thing or a drainage ditch modified to look like a Venetian canal. Those that weren't on the water overlooked a golf course. The golfing pants known as "plus fours" were the uniform of the hour for real estate salesmen. "Subdivision orator" was considered a job description, and William Jennings Bryan's voice was the loudest of all.

Voices like his were required because so much was based on faith and vision. You had to look at it through their eyes rather than your own, because yours would tell you that instead of elegant clubhouses and Mediterranean villas and yacht basins and golf courses, you were actually looking at mudflats and swampland and palmetto scrub and cow pastures. The emperor, indeed, had no clothes. But there were few to point it out because the will to believe was almost as strong as the will to grow rich, and one depended upon the other.

It was an age of superlatives. Everything could be made better, and surely would—at least on paper.

St. Augustine was slow to get in on the act, but it was not immune to the lure of profit. The stories from elsewhere were reprinted here. Why should our real estate market languish when fortunes were being made overnight in Miami and Tampa and elsewhere?

The creation of land used to be seen as the province of God, but by the 1920s he had a helping hand from a whole slew of Florida developers who performed miracles not with loaves and fishes but with dredges, fill, and draglines. One of the kings

Los Robles

Some houses have not only addresses but also names, and Los Robles (Spanish for "The Oaks," as it is located in the midst of the North City live oak grove) at 24 Nelmar Avenue fully justifies the distinction. It was built for Ruth Hopkins Shackford Pickering from Duluth, Minnesota, who grew up as part of the wealthy winter colony in St. Augustine and died tragically in a 1944 fire at Marjorie Kinnan Rawlings' penthouse in the Castle Warden Hotel. In the spring of 1924 she was traveling in California and became impressed with the work of Pasadena's Wallace Neff (1895–1982), known as "the architect to the stars." She had him design this house, which offers a southwestern slant on boomtime architecture with its inward sloping walls and soft corners reminiscent of adobe construction. A picturesque exterior staircase to a second-floor bedroom is a notable design feature, as is its com-

position in four segments, curving around the corner of two streets.

Poet Edna St. Vincent Millay was a guest here in 1935, visiting her friend Terry MacGovern. There is a small irony here, as MacGovern was divorced from Mildred Harris, the first wife of Charlie Chaplin, and Chaplin hired Wallace Neff to design a home for him in California. Other movie clients of the architect included Darryl Zanuck, Mary Pickford, Cary Grant, King Vidor, and Groucho, Harpo, and Gummo Marx.

24 NELMAR AVENUE

Who Started This?

Often we hear the question asked, "Who started the boom in St. Augustine?" Various people are claiming credit for turning the trick. The *Evening Record* does not know who started it, but we do know that there is no man in all the world powerful enough to stop it. Like the Florida boom, it is here to stay; and the bottom is so well riveted in that it cannot fall out.

—Editorial, *St. Augustine Evening Record,*
March 13, 1925

among these was a Green Cove Springs native named D. P. Davis. "Doc" Davis made his name—and an impressive paper fortune—by pumping islands out of the bay in Tampa and selling them to seemingly endless lines of enthusiastic buyers.

A couple of local movers and shakers knew Davis and his major-domo, A. Y. Milam, and let them know there was a piece of property where the same thing could be done in St. Augustine. Pretty soon the Ancient City was in there with every other town, development, ex-turpentine camp and former dump site in Florida, having its charms hyped to the world.

The marshy north end of Anastasia Island was to become "Davis Shores" in the rechristened "St. Augustine on the Ocean"—with the promise that its hotel, Roman pool, casino, yacht club, golf courses, country club, and endless miles of canals would make it "America's foremost watering place."

The sales brochure began not with a fulsome description of the land and amenities, however, but jumped right to the bottom line as the attention grabber: "Following D. P. Davis for Big Quick Real Estate Profits."

A hefty special issue of the newspaper modestly hailed Davis's arrival, placing him squarely in the footsteps of Ponce de León, Pedro Menéndez, and Henry Flagler. He was to spend $60,000,000 and employ 3,000 people—truly music to the ears of Ancient Citians. The Kiwanis Club took out a full page

48 SEVILLA STREET

One of the most elegant houses of the 1920s boom has a history older than its looks. 48 Sevilla Street was originally a wooden Victorian building facing King Street, built after the Civil War and known as the Anderson Cottage after its owners, who made their home next door at Markland. It was rented to many people, including W. W. Dewhurst, who wrote the pioneering *The History of St. Augustine, Florida* (1881). When Henry Flagler bought the eastern end of the Markland property to build his grand Ponce de Leon Hotel, this cottage was moved a few feet northwest to its current location. There it continued to house a variety of winter residents, including author Rebecca Ruter Springer (1832–1904), wife of the Indiana congressman who sponsored statehood for Washington, Montana, and the Dakotas. The Anderson family itself occupied the cottage in 1899–1900 while Markland was being enlarged and remodeled.

During the 1920s boom, 48 Sevilla was remodeled in the Mediterranean Revival style by architect Fred A. Henderich, who gave it his typical shell-dash stucco finish. An episode of the popular television series *Route 66* was filmed here in 1964.

ad to state its belief that "Not only has D. P. Davis builded beauty spots out of wildernesses and lifted fairy gardens and ideal home sites from the depths of the sea itself, but he has withal builded a good name—a reputation for fair dealing, public service, unselfish effort and high integrity."

Since visiting the site itself could hardly be inspirational (the "world's largest dredging project" had not yet turned it into high ground), an elaborate model of what Davis Shores *would* look like was built on Aviles Street, and buyers were quick to accept the projection as reality and plunk their money down.

Davis was not the only big name who figured in boomtime St. Augustine. New York millionaire August Heckscher could look across the water at Davis Shores from his own development, Vilano Beach, which featured similar curving streets. He kept a private apartment in the Vilano Beach Casino, where the swimming pool featured saltwater in the summer and artesian well water in the winter. It was built by Matthew Hasbrouck who would, a few years later, put a swimming pool in the White House for President Franklin Roosevelt—after which he returned to St. Augustine to construct the original tanks at Marineland.

It was not only outsiders who stoked the fires of the Boom: a whole host of local lawyers, dentists, realtors, merchants, and military officers got into the act as well. Even high school students dropped out to make their fortunes in something more immediately profitable than algebra.

The area was dotted with new developments: Santa Rosa, Saratoga Lake, Coquina Gables, Orenda, Vermont Heights, Fort Moosa Gardens, Araquay Park, Parque Aviles, Menendez Park, Seminole Heights, Aiken Park, and so on. Part of the sales pitch was in the name. If it could convey Spanish or Polynesian or Venetian fantasies, or suggest attributes (often bogus) related to water, shrubbery, or high land, so much the better. For pure *chutzpah*, nothing surpassed the low-lying Gold Mine Heights, which hasn't produced a nugget from that day to this. Real names like Trestle Bay Swamp or Mosquito Inlet or Rattlesnake Island were nowhere to be seen in the real estate advertisements of the time: it was not an age in which ecology sold.

All these contemplated paradises, of course, were for whites only. The United States Supreme Court had

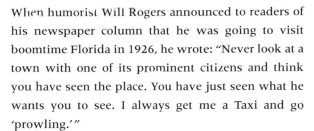

Will Rogers in St. Augustine

When humorist Will Rogers announced to readers of his newspaper column that he was going to visit boomtime Florida in 1926, he wrote: "Never look at a town with one of its prominent citizens and think you have seen the place. You have just seen what he wants you to see. I always get me a Taxi and go 'prowling.'"

Sure enough, after his visit to the Ancient City in February, it was reported:

"Rogers and his company arrived at noon yesterday from Jacksonville over the road 'designed by an architect who had a motorcycle,' gave everybody the slip, caught a taxi and saw St. Augustine, taking in the fort, the oldest house, the alligators and the fountain of youth. 'I just ooze tradition,' he declared. He said he was afraid that if a committee caught him, it would insist on showing him lots which doubled in value overnight."

ruled some of the earlier approaches to residential segregation unconstitutional, so by the 1920s deed restrictions and restrictive covenants had become the favorite devices. The one included by Davis Shores in its sales contracts read as follows: "No part of said lands or any interest therein shall be given, loaned, rented, leased, encumbered or conveyed to any person of negro blood."

Persons of that blood could go to the Washington Street office of Frank Butler and purchase a lot in College Park, "The Colored Subdivision Superb." Sales contracts for those lots included no deed restrictions.

During the Boom, one thing fed another. The spirit of the times increased the number of realtors, and they all needed offices. Places that had previously sheltered low-budget artists or antique shoppes were quickly spiffed up and turned into real estate offices. All the new developments had to be advertised, and the once-thin *St. Augustine Evening Record* grew fatter and fatter: from one section to two to three. All the buyers had to make financial arrangements, and this increased business for the banks, which expanded accordingly. They enlarged, remodeled, and—in one case—built the city's only skyscraper.

Many of the new real estate projects were on the other side of the river, so new bridges were built to reach them. The million-dollar Bridge of Lions to Davis Shores was hailed as "the most beautiful bridge in Dixie." St. Augustine had anticipated the Boom in 1923 by expanding its city limits: all the new developments expected municipal services as well.

Signs of mania should have been obvious to the impartial observer, but there were few to be impartial with all the paper fortunes being made in 1925.

Then reality paused to take a breath.

As 1926 progressed, the frenzy cooled a bit. It was the period of "silly slump talk."

D. P. Davis went on the offensive with his well-oiled publicity machine. In a full-page ad in *The New York Times* and other leading newspapers, he tried to set the Doubting Thomases straight. There would be no bust, he (or his ghostwriter) pointed out, because there was, in fact, no boom. It was merely a case of real estate prices that had previously been depressed now rising to their natural value. It was happening due to a

confluence of factors: the growth of the automobile and highways; the wider availability of electricity; national prosperity and its distribution down the social scale; Florida's climate and the establishment of the winter vacation habit; and the development of modern advertising, publicity, and salesmanship.

The man who had recently sold $19,000,000 worth of lots on Davis Shores in a single day informed the nation that "I regard the prices at which lots have been

5 TREMERTON STREET

OWEN D. YOUNG HOUSE   The waterfront home at 5 Tremerton Street, with its distinctive green tile roof, was designed by architect Fred Henderich for A. E. Pilgrim, who owned a local shoe store. The Pilgrim family moved in just a week before the 1926 hurricane decisively swept away the Florida land boom. In later years it was the home of Owen D. Young, chairman of the board of General Electric, founder of the Radio Corporation of America, and *Time* magazine's Man of the Year for 1929. He and his second wife, Louise, had a winter home at what is now Washington Oaks State Gardens, but as he became quite elderly, he stayed in this house, which was conveniently located just a few feet from Flagler Hospital. Owen D. Young died here on July 11, 1962, at the age of 87.

124 MARINE STREET

THE MURDER HOUSE   St. Augustinians picked up their afternoon paper one day in January 1974 to read the banner headline "Former Mayor's Wife Hacked to Death." Thus did the substantial boom-period dwelling at 124 Marine Street come to be known as the Murder House for the grisly event that took place on its front steps. Athalia Ponsell, a 55-year-old former John Powers model and Republican political activist, had recently taken as her fourth husband former Mayor James Lindsley, who described her as a "great American patriot, scornful of governmental extravagance, waste and chicanery whether it lurked in local or federal government." Her next-door neighbor, the county manager whom she had attempted to get fired, was tried and acquitted for the murder, which remains officially unsolved.

Boom Houses

The handful of buildings actually constructed in Davis Shores included both private homes like 10 Montrano Avenue, with its three-stepped roof and metal balcony, and apartment houses like 12 Arpieka Avenue with its articulated door surrounds. Architect for the Davis projects was Carlos Schoeppl of Hedrick & Schoeppl, who also designed the Vilano Beach Casino for August Heckscher. In North City's Fullerwood neighborhood, a streetcar suburb whose original development ceased with the outbreak of World War I, there was an infill of boom-period construction like the house at 52 Bay View Drive designed by F. A. Hollingsworth.

10 MONTRANO AVENUE

12 ARPIEKA AVENUE

52 BAY VIEW DRIVE

Architects' Own Houses

The two leading architects to practice in St. Augustine in the first half of the 20th century were Fred A. Henderich (1879–1941) and Francis A. Hollingsworth (1885–1974).

Henderich, a native of New York City and graduate of Columbia University, came to St. Augustine in 1905 to work for the Florida East Coast Hotel Company and later went into private practice. In what is probably a typical architect's story, Henderich's father-in-law owned a large piece of land on south St. George Street, and the architect was able to design many of the houses that went up there. He excelled at bungalow design, using native wood shingles, palm tree porch posts, and coquina stone fireplaces.

He also pioneered the Mediterranean Revival style in Florida, designing such landmarks as the Plaza Bandstand, Flagler Hospital, Florida Normal College, Excelsior School, Hastings High School, and the Visitors Center. In this work he frequently used a stucco finish with coquina shell dash as a particular local element.

F. A. Hollingsworth was a Virginian who came here to work for the Florida East Coast Railway, then opened his own office in 1922. His work is visible in St. Augustine's only skyscraper: the bank building on the plaza. He also designed the Florida East Coast Railway headquarters on Malaga Street and the synagogue on Cordova Street. He was a pioneer restoration architect, working on St. Francis Barracks after it was gutted by fire in 1916. In Hastings, he designed the Civic Center and the Potato Growers building.

One place that combines the work of both Hollingsworth and Henderich is the St. Augustine Record Building at Bridge and Cordova Streets. Henderich designed the original building in 1906, and Hollingsworth designed the addition to the south, as well as overall remodeling, in the 1920s.

What did these architects choose for their own homes during the Boom?

Henderich bought 297 St. George Street in 1925. It was a house he had designed for a client back in 1914, making it one of the earliest examples of what would become the boom's commonest style. The local press noted, "It has been, since its completion, the center of much attention for those interested in the Spanish type of architecture, and remains one of the most attractive homes in the city."

Hollingsworth took a small, turn-of-the-century wood frame house at 35 Valencia Street (choicely located across from the Presbyterian Church and Kirkside, the Flagler estate) and remodeled and enlarged it to suit his needs. The final result, with dramatic sections of exposed coquina in the chimney, bears many resemblances to the corner of the Vaill Block at Cathedral Place and Charlotte Street that he remodeled at the same time for a bank. (In recent years it has been St. Augustine's leading bookstore, The Booksmith.) The ornamental chimney cap is similar to the one on 124 Marine Street.

297 ST GEORGE STREET

35 VALENCIA STREET

and are being sold in the better class of developments as being generally far below actual values." So buy up!

But the bloom was off the rose. The period known as "the lull" was entered. Then in September 1926 a hurricane blew it all away. Though Florida newspapers, so used to peddling only good news about their state, persisted in referring to it as "the gale," the rest of the country's press did not give it such kid-glove treatment, and in its aftermath the only purchasers of Florida real estate were sharks in search of rock-bottom prices—and there weren't even very many of them.

"Subdivision orators" decamped for Wall Street, real estate offices closed, newspapers shrank, banks started to go under, swollen cities sought to shed their excess acreage and defaulted on their bonds, another hurricane hit, then a freeze and a citrus blight. When it rains it pours.

After the stock market crash of 1929, prosperity became a faded memory for the entire nation.

The remains of D. P. Davis's multimillion-dollar dream were auctioned off on the courthouse steps in 1933. They brought less than $10,000.

Doc was not around to see it. He departed as spectacularly as he had arrived. Less than a month after the 1926 hurricane, he went out the porthole of an ocean liner in the middle of the Atlantic. A banner headline proclaimed "D. P. DAVIS DROWNS AT SEA," followed by "Affairs Were in Good Shape. Davis Shores to Carry On."

Only the first part was true.

CHAPTER SEVEN

Modern Times

BUTLER'S BEACH

Single-family beach houses became an endangered species in parts of Florida during the 1970s with the rush to put together parcels of property to build condominiums. Doubly endangered were the historic black beaches from the era of segregation. One of them was just south of St. Augustine: Butler's Beach, established by Frank B. Butler (1885–1973) after the collapse of the 1920s land boom. Streets there were named for members of the Butler family. This view is looking north on Gloria Avenue between Minnie Street and Mary Street. The homes in the foreground are part of the original settlement; the condominium in the background was built on what had previously been part of Butler's Beach. There needs to be a concerted effort to preserve the historic black beaches of Florida and get them listed on the National Register of Historic Places before they vanish forever.

THE GIDDINESS OF THE BOOM was followed by two decades of very little building. First there was the Great Depression, when poverty was a drawback, and then World War II when restrictions on all kinds of building materials that were channeled into military use made it difficult to launch a private construction project even in the face of growing prosperity.

Still, those decades did manage to leave their architectural mark. The alphabet soup agencies of the New Deal—FERA, CWA, PWA, and WPA—provided construction jobs for the unemployed and resulted in buildings like the coquina Visitors Center, Government House on the Plaza (originally a post office), and facilities like the airport, located conveniently on a failed boomtime subdivision.

The economic hardships of the Depression also sparked the first widespread interest in a historic preservation program for the Oldest City. Much publicity had attended the efforts of John D. Rockefeller, Jr., to recreate Colonial Williamsburg and of Henry Ford's establishment of Greenfield Village, which brought together historic artifacts and buildings in Dearborn, Michigan. St. Augustine's go-getter Mayor Walter B. Fraser, owner of the Fountain of Youth and dealer in historic properties, felt that capitalizing on the Ancient City's past might be the road to prosperity for its future. All that was lacking was a Ford or Rockefeller to underwrite the effort. The closest they could come up with was the Carnegie Institution of Washington, which bore the name of a famous—but, alas, long-dead—millionaire.

Things started with great fanfare, with prestigious advisory committees, first-rate historic research, archaeological investigation, and the formulation of plans. The program contained within it the contradiction between serious historic work and the promotion of gimcrack tourism, and its more ambitious visions soon outran its resources. If the outbreak of World War II didn't kill it, then it certainly put it in the deep freeze. But it was a sustained effort that mobilized the community, educated its people, and created a consciousness that old buildings could be treasures as well as trash. It would bear much fruit in succeeding decades.

First, however, came the war. St. Augustine's hotels were taken over by the Coast Guard for training purposes: a good thing since travel restrictions, ra-

6600 BROWARD STREET

MARJORIE KINNAN RAWLINGS BEACH HOUSE   One of Florida's most significant literary landmarks is the cottage at 6600 Broward Street in Crescent Beach that Pulitzer Prize–winning novelist Marjorie Kinnan Rawlings (1896–1953) purchased in 1939 with money made from *The Yearling.* It had been built by Ralph Poole, one of the founders of Marineland, and was called Goat Hill, because he had a goat tethered there to keep the lawn trimmed. Rawlings' friend (and eventual literary executor) Julia Scribner rechristened the place Crawlings-by-the-Sea, after the plentiful local spiders which terrified her.

Rawlings worked here on *Cross Creek* (1942), *Cross Creek Cookery* (1942), and her final novel, *The Sojourner* (1953). This was the setting for one of her favorite short stories, "The Pelican's Shadow." Guests here over the years included Robert Frost, Ernest Hemingway, Zora Neale Hurston, and Dylan Thomas. This was the novelist's main home during the last decade of her life. She and her husband, Norton Baskin, had the place greatly enlarged in the 1940s.

Threatened with demolition during the 1980s so that two houses could be built on the valuable beachfront property, Crawlings-by-the-Sea was dramatically saved at the last minute by Mary Elizabeth Streeter of Indianapolis, Indiana. She was an admirer of Rawlings' work from her own experience as a teacher of children's literature. Floridians will always be grateful that she rescued this important part of our cultural heritage from thoughtless destruction.

tioning of gas and tires, and a coastal blackout would have destroyed the tourist business for the duration. Tents sprang up like mushrooms just north of the city gates to accommodate visiting soldiers. They couldn't see all the local attractions; Marineland, then the newest, had closed down for the war. Its grounds were used to train patrol dogs, and its scientists applied their skills to the development of shark repellent to help downed aviators. But the Alligator Farm remained open and did a booming business, as did the bars. Novelist James Branch Cabell, a longtime winter

A L'aise

The estate called A L'aise (French for "At Ease") at 400 Old Quarry Road was built in 1929 by contractor Goold T. Butler for New York millionaire August Heckscher (1848–1941). A German immigrant, Heckscher made his first fortune in coal and zinc mining and his second in real estate (the Heckscher Building at Fifth Avenue and 57th Street is one of the Big Apple's landmarks). A famous philanthropist, he started the Heckscher Foundation for Children and bought a Florida orange grove to help feed the poor of New York. In later years, Heckscher's birthday parties were regularly covered by the press. At 90 he declared, "This used to be a great country before we had the income tax." At 91 he said that Hitler was "the greatest man alive today" and doubted there would be another world war. A week later, Hitler invaded Poland and the war was on.

Local legend goes that the "No 400" on the gatepost of this estate does not mean "Number 400" (though that has come to be its address over the years), but rather that none of the elite 400 of New York society were welcome therein, because of some slight.

The grounds of A L'aise included an orange grove (and, in modern times, a bomb shelter), and the house itself was picturesquely built around a swimming pool. Guarding the pool is a wrought-iron gate brought from Italy. When it proved to be not wide enough for the opening, a local artisan was found to create matching panels to the left and right of the originals.

For many decades after Heckscher's departure, A L'aise was home to the family of Hobson T. Cone, owner of Zoric Cleaners and one-time mayor of St. Augustine.

Looking Backward

4400 Coastal Highway

70 Water Street

St. Augustine has not been on the cutting edge of modern architecture. Many of the most interesting houses of modern times look backward rather than forward for their design inspiration. The multisided beach house at 4400 Coastal Highway is a virtual reproduction of the popular screw-pile lighthouses built in Chesapeake Bay in the decades after the Civil War.

The dignified shingled house at 70 Water Street, designed by architect F. A. Hollingsworth in 1935 for J. W. Hoffman, head of Henry Flagler's Model Land Company, is a good example of the long-popular Colonial Revival style. It was home, during the early 1940s, to Meredith Nicholson (1866–1947), the famous Indiana novelist who wrote *The House of a Thousand Candles* (1905) and spent the decade prior to his Ancient City sojourn as an American diplomat in Latin America.

resident, wrote that the town was "filled every Saturday evening with forlorn drunken children. They have not even the heart to become boisterous, but merely drink themselves into stupor and extreme nausea. The spectacle I do not find exhilarating."

Groups of Texas soldiers became famous for going into bars, playing "Deep in the Heart of Texas" on the jukebox, and insisting that everyone either stand at attention or fight. They kept the military police busy.

Some of the county's agricultural crops were harvested by German prisoners of war, replacing the labor of local men gone off to fight.

The Signal Corps established its only training facility for African-Americans in St. Augustine at Florida Normal College. They were the corps' counterpart of the famous "Tuskegee Airmen."

The war ushered in an era of prosperity, but restrictions were not eased immediately with the end of fighting. The story is told of a man who wanted to build some cottages at Vilano Beach and knew a dealer

who had the lumber but was not permitted to sell it. However, he was told, "I'll sell you this pencil here for $5,000, and you can have all the wood you want for nothing."

Eventually these glitches worked out and construction started up again. It was a great relief to the returning servicemen, at long last reunited with their wives, who had been forced to worry about squeaking bedsprings when sharing cramped quarters with relatives on ending their duty.

Immediately favored by the turn of events was Davis Shores, whose many vacant lots were "only 2200 feet from downtown St. Augustine," as D. P. Davis' flacks had pointed out years before.

Others headed to the beach, where building lots running from ocean to river could be had for $1,000 each. The government advertised that leftover Quonset huts would make excellent beach cottages, and many bought and moved them at low prices.

If the architecture of the preceding era had been

The St. Augustine Colonial Revival Style

The restoration and reconstruction activities of the 1960s led to the development of what Robert Harper has named the St. Augustine Colonial Revival style. Examples of it run the gamut from remodeled (or "Spanished-up") older buildings, to academically correct new construction in old styles, to a few arches and clay tiles added to the front of a grocery store rising out of a blacktopped parking lot. The results may be ingenious, attractive, insipid, or downright tacky.

In some ways, Walter B. Fraser, owner of the Fountain of Youth and mayor during the 1930s, could be considered the spiritual ancestor of the style; he prided himself on the ability to make buildings look older than they were.

In its 1960s version, leading popularizers and practitioners included architect James Gamble Rogers of Winter Park; Earle Newton, first director of what became the Historic St. Augustine Preservation Board; and contractors William Forrester and E. B. Meade.

A similar approach has long been taken to new construction in the old Spanish city of Santa Fe, New Mexico. Pictured here are examples of houses in the St. Augustine Colonial Revival style.

19 Park Terrace Drive

24 Avista Circle

43 Cordova Street

111 Shores Boulevard

The Deltona Corporation's St. Augustine Shores development was the quintessential cookie-cutter subdivision of modern times. Even here there are buildings that will attract future attention. My son Hamilton, a great baseball fan, thinks there should be a historic marker on 111 Shores Boulevard. It was home in the early 1970s to baseball great Johnny Mize (1913–1993). "The Big Cat," as he was known, hit 51 home runs in 1947, led the National League in batting in 1939, and was a seven-time All Star. In 1981 he was elected to the Baseball Hall of Fame.

18 North St. Augustine Boulevard

THE FIRST CONDO Condominium is technically a form of property ownership, applicable to many different types of property, but in Florida it has come to mean primarily beachfront buildings stuffed like sardine cans, representing man's symbolic conquest of nature. The first condo in St. Augustine, named Colonia en la Bahia (Spanish for "colony on the bay"), was neither beachfront nor high-rise. It is located at 18 North St. Augustine Boulevard on Davis Shores, near the Bridge of Lions, and was designed in the early 1970s by our pioneer female architect, Lea Wells. One of the notable occupants was Clarissa Anderson Gibbs, who could remember sitting on Henry Flagler's lap as a child, and who continued until her death at 94 in 1990 the role of public benefactor begun by her father, Dr. Andrew Anderson of Markland.

grandiose, that of the postwar period could only be described as insipid. Future generations will no doubt find charms in it, this being the unvarying lesson of historic preservation, but for now the appeal seems elusive.

It was an age of cookie-cutter subdivisions, with houses like those that inspired Malvina Reynolds' classic song "Little Boxes." Sidewalk superintendents of any seniority could see the diminution in solidity of building materials, which went from real wood to plywood to chipboard to something that looks like cardboard covered with tinfoil and gives little reassurance that some Big Bad Wolf could not huff and puff and blow the house down.

Since the buildings themselves were not much to look at, they sprouted picture windows to take in the outside views, then sliding-glass doors, which became so generic that builders did not hesitate to put them in walls that overlooked scenic interstate highways.

Air conditioning became a standard amenity and wrought a revolution in architecture, making porches obsolete and large windows energy-inefficient.

Transportation was likewise revolutionized, first by cutting U.S. 1 along the San Sebastian River like an

angry scar, and then by building Interstate 95 a few miles to the west. Both left in their wake a litter of yesterday's hotels, motels, guest homes, and tourist camps, deprived of the lifeblood of being on the main route of travel.

The modern age brought different housing aggregates as well.

At the beach, the old single-family cottages were increasingly replaced by condominiums, which featured all the rusticity and informality of an urban apartment house. Hundreds, even thousands, now frolicked where two or three had previously enjoyed the wildness and solitude.

In the old days, a community was a kind of social whole, including an elite as well as the village idiot and town drunk. To grow up in these places was to become familiar with a whole range of humanity. As the twentieth century approached its end, there was an increasing attempt to separate the classes, using guard-gated communities occupied by homogenized people. These new social organisms will surely develop their own pathologies and tragedies in years to come.

Each generation has its own way of disrespecting the architecture of the preceding one. This is the danger period for that particular style. Buildings may be stripped of ornamentation, or have their original windows yanked out with all the delicacy of a dentist pulling teeth without anesthesia. Different building materials may be grafted on: metal windows instead of wood-framed ones, hollow core doors instead of paneled ones.

Or the whole thing may be covered up. Asbestos shingles, stucco, aluminum or vinyl siding, fake brick, and cast stone have all been peddled by boiler-room operators promising a life free of hassles to the unwary homeowner. The dinner hour of St. Augustinians is regularly interrupted by telephone hawkers doing their best to make a dollar by further damaging the historic fabric of the city.

The organized historic preservation movement returned to St. Augustine with the economic slump of the late 1950s. A delegation of community leaders went to Williamsburg to see how it was done and decided to transplant the experience here, with state money substituting for that of the Rockefellers. A frequently heard description, that St. Augustine is a Spanish Colonial Williamsburg, shows an obvious inferiority complex. This being the oldest city, why should Williamsburg not be considered a British Colonial St. Augustine?

Property was acquired in the St. George Street area and buildings of the colonial era began to be restored or reconstructed. This gave rise to two interesting contradictions in the 1960s.

The first was the idea of preservation by bulldozer. Many Victorian buildings—some of serious architectural and historic significance—were destroyed to make way for imitation colonial structures. The result was the creation of a busy tourist district on St. George Street specializing in T-shirts and rubber alligators. In ensuing decades, property became so valuable that buildings were increasingly subdivided into mini-malls, featuring all the essential consumer goods that have everywhere given rise to the term "tourist trap." This one masquerades in pseudo-Spanish colonial garb, and some still insist that the process has been a major contribution to history. A favorite oxymoronic term in St. Augustine is "authentic reproduction."

When we conducted the survey of old buildings that originally set me to walking the streets of the Ancient City, the thickest file we accumulated was that of buildings demolished between 1959 and 1978—hundreds and hundreds of them, many real heartbreakers.

It reached such scandalous proportions that the Friends of St. Augustine Architecture was formed in 1979 to try to put an end to the carnage. Its efforts were valiant, if sometimes unavailing, but at least the malefactors knew that some opposition could be expected. The era of graveyard silence had ended. The bulldozers did not cease, but at least throttled back their speed.

In the 1950s and 1960s books were written advising the stripping of gingerbread from Victorian houses to render them ersatz modern. By the 1990s, while some of those ideas survived, it was increasingly likely that "gussying-up" would be a threat to the integrity of architecture.

Bungalows that hadn't had the first nail driven into them until two decades after Queen Victoria's death all of a sudden sprouted with gingerbread that they never saw in their original incarnation, frequently with a coat of pink paint added for good measure.

Leaded, beveled, etched, and stained glass in patterns never seen here—not even in the grand hotels where the work was done by Louis Comfort Tiffany—made a visually overwhelming appearance here a century late and a continent away from their natural home.

All these changes may have been made with the best of intentions and in the interests of brightening up the area. But what is lost in the process is the authentic architecture of the nation's oldest city—and that is no small loss indeed.

The second great contradiction to come out of the 1960s was between being a place where history is peddled and being the place where history is actually made.

In 1964 St. Augustine was preparing for the celebration of its 400th birthday. An outdoor amphitheatre with a new state play written by Pulitzer-prizewinner Paul Green was one of the projects. Another was a 208-foot stainless steel cross and an ultra-modern church on the grounds of the Mission of Nombre de Dios. The face of downtown was starting to step back in time due to restoration, bulldozing, and reconstruction. People

Castle Otttis

3 3RD STREET, NORTH BEACH

Rising like a mirage out of the low-slung beach trees west of the coastal highway is an imposing structure inspired by an Irish castle of a thousand years ago, and dedicated to Jesus Christ. Built by musician Rusty Ickes and two friends between 1984 and 1990, it has no heat, no plumbing, and no electricity. Its four towers are lined with curving rustic staircases, and from the top you can see all the way to the lighthouse and downtown St. Augustine. The main room in the multilevel interior is a chapel, complete with sawdust on the floor. Fluorescent lights (run from an extension cord) shed a bluish glow through the open windows at night. Chiseled in granite, at the doorstep, is a quote from Victorian tastemaker John Ruskin which begins, "When we build, let us think that we build forever. . . ." Much of the building material (mostly rough-faced concrete block) was donated from builders' overruns. It is open one Sunday a month to benefit local charities, and many weddings have been held in the chapel.

looked forward to a great party and a lot of tourist-generated prosperity.

That year, 1964, was also the time when the civil rights movement was challenging the racial mores of the country. There were protests against segregation in courthouses, churches, schools, hospitals, restaurants, motels, movie theaters, restrooms, and elsewhere, and discrimination in all facets of American life.

The civil rights movement came together with St. Augustine's 400th birthday, and the results were explosive. When local rights leaders like Dr. Robert Hayling and Henry L. Twine convinced Dr. Martin Luther King to come to the Ancient City, it became a major battlefield—the last great campaign of Dr. King that led to the passage of the landmark Civil Rights Act of 1964 which outlawed segregation practices all over the country and served as an inspiration to the rest of the world. Perhaps never in all its centuries did events in St. Augustine have such a wide impact. Yet, even a quarter of a century later there was a curious reticence on the part of some to acknowledge that it even happened.

Martin Luther King Slept Here

156 MARTIN LUTHER KING AVENUE

5718 RUDOLPH AVENUE

Given the violent temper of the time, it was considered unsafe for Martin Luther King to spend more than one night in the same house during his visits to St. Augustine at the time of the demonstrations that led to the passage of the landmark Civil Rights Act of 1964. In the ironic way that history has of turning around, this offers the future possibility of a whole series of "Martin Luther King Slept Here" signs, not unlike those "George Washington Slept Here" markers that dot other parts of the country.

Of course, this presupposes that all the sites will be pinpointed while memories still remain. Before his death in 1994, Henry Twine—who was the heart and soul of the civil rights movement in St. Augustine—showed me several of the places. The house at 156 Martin Luther King Avenue points up the fact that not all of our historic buildings are of antique vintage. Many communities now have streets named for Dr. King; I have always considered ours to be special because he actually walked on it in the course of making history. The house at 5718 Rudolph Avenue in Butler's Beach has been moved and enlarged since King's time. In keeping with the fate of beach property, a condominium has been built on the original site.

Henry Twine also pointed out 81 and 83 Bridge Street as houses where King stayed in 1964.

St. Augustinians learned that it can be traumatic to be the place where history is actually made. While it was some people's finest hour, it was others' worst. By contrast, peddling history's trinkets and souvenirs is easy.

But a hundred years from now, people will remember the protester and forget the peddler. Tourists of that time will ask where the demonstrations took place, not where the rubber alligators were sold.

Sometimes the easy things just don't have the longest lifespan.

That may not be a bad lesson to draw from looking over the past four-plus centuries of St. Augustine's history.

168 Avenida Menendez

400 Old Quarry Road

262 St. George Street

234 St. George Street

334 Charlotte Street

143 Cordova Street

234 St. George Street

and Gates

15 BRIDGE STREET

38 CARRERA STREET

38 CARRERA STREET

7 BRIDGE STREET

52 ST. GEORGE STREET

EPILOGUE

IN 1985 A POWERFUL INSTITUTION, KNOWN for boasting of the millions of dollars it pumped into the local economy, wanted to bulldoze four of the finest Flagler-era houses in St. Augustine.

An eight-year-old girl, having memorized a favorite poem, decided to recite it at the public hearing where various permissions would or would not be granted for what had come to be called the Saturday Night Massacre.

The institution was represented by the highest-priced legal talent in town. The little girl had only a page torn from one of her children's magazines. She proceeded boldly to the microphone, dressed in her Sunday best, and recited Rachel Field's poem:

> I like old houses best, don't you?
> They never go cluttering up a view
> With roofs too red and paint too new,
> With doors too green and blinds too blue!
> The old ones look as if they grew,
> Their bricks may be dingy, their clapboards askew
> From sitting so many seasons through,
> But they've learned in a hundred years or two
> Not to go cluttering up a view!

Representatives of the institution blustered about "allegedly historic buildings," spoke of large sums of money, and issued veiled threats, but the final score was:

little girl   3
powerful institution   1

One interesting building was sacrificed on the altar of "progress," but three were saved to delight the eyes of tourists and townspeople alike, hopefully for centuries to come.

That little girl might have stayed home that night and played games or watched television. Instead she did her duty as a citizen in a way that put many of her elders to shame—and left future generations of citizens in her debt.

I am doubly proud of that girl whose poetry recitation helped save those houses, because she is my daughter, Sudie.

May our Ancient City—and many other cities not so ancient—always have a plentiful supply of Sudies willing to stand up to preserve our historic buildings.

There is much buck-passing in the world. "It's not my responsibility" is the excuse heard over and over again.

Ah, but it is. Just as the ethics of citizenship require that we not spit on the sidewalks nor dump our garbage in the streets nor poison our water supply with hazardous chemicals, so too are we obligated to do our share to preserve our heritage and pass it on as undiminished as possible to our heirs.

FURTHER READING

The literature on St. Augustine is vast, if still incomplete. The finest collection of it is in the St. Augustine Historical Society Library, an institution that is one of the great treasures of the Ancient City. To live here without being familiar with it is to miss an essential part of the experience; to visit and fail to see it is to leave a gap in your education.

I hesitate, out of the vastness, to start recommending works for fear of leaving others out. Let me just say that Albert Manucy's classic *The Houses of St. Augustine 1565–1821* (St. Augustine Historical Society, 1962) and Karen Harvey's two volumes, *St. Augustine and St. Johns County: A Pictorial History (Donning Company, 1980),* and *America's First City: St. Augustine's Historic Neighborhoods* (Tailored Tours Publications, 1992) all touch on the subject matter of this book. Among the many volumes on broader aspects of the Ancient City's history, I have always considered Thomas Graham's *The Awakening of St. Augustine* (St. Augustine Historical Society, 1978) to be a model of diligence in research and clarity in writing. Of my own *Fifty Feet in Paradise: The Booming of Florida* (Harcourt Brace Jovanovich, 1984), let me say modestly that one could scarcely be considered a Floridian—hardly even a tourist—without having committed large portions of it to memory.

Everything exists in a context, and the would-be connoisseur of St. Augustine's architecture over the centuries should become familiar with American architectural literature in general. Russell Lynes, *The Tastemakers* (Harper & Brothers, 1954); Wayne Andrews, *Architecture, Ambition and Americans* (Free Press, 1964); and James Marston Fitch, *American Building: The Forces That Shape It* (Houghton Mifflin, 1948), all provide readable introductions.

The architecture of the Sunshine State is dealt with

in Hap Hatton, *Tropical Splendor* (Knopf, 1987); Beth Dunlop, *Florida's Vanishing Architecture* (Pineapple Press, 1987); and Ron Haase, *Classic Cracker: Florida's Wood-Frame Vernacular Architecture* (Pineapple Press, 1992).

A variety of books provide information on particular styles: Roger G. Kennedy, *Greek Revival America* (Stewart, Tabori & Chang, 1989); Alma McArdle, *Carpenter Gothic* (Whitney Library of Design, 1978); Wayne Andrews, *American Gothic* (Random House, 1975); William B. Rhoads, *The Colonial Revival* (Garland, 1977); Vincent Scully, *The Shingle Style and the Stick Style* (Yale University Press, 1971); and Clay Lancaster, *The American Bungalow* (Abbeville Press, 1985).

Pictures are still worth a thousand words, and we are blessed with a large shelf of works that show buildings in all their splendor. My own favorites include:

John Maass, *The Gingerbread Age* (Rinehart, 1957); Clay Lancaster, *Architectural Follies in America* (C.E. Tuttle, 1960); Ben Karp, *Ornamental Carpentry on Nineteenth Century American Houses* (Dover Publications, 1981); and the popular series by Elizabeth Pomada and Michael Larsen: *Painted Ladies* (Dutton, 1978); *Daughters of Painted Ladies* (Dutton, 1987); *The Painted Ladies Revisited* (Dutton, 1989); and *How to Create Your Own Painted Lady* (Dutton, 1989).

Good architecture delights the eye, exalts the soul, and engages the mind. A number of well-written polemics remind us that architecture should be part of the public debate, and that we ignore it at our peril. For a little mental stimulation, try Brent Brolin, *Architecture in Context* (Van Nostrand Reinhold, 1980), and *The Failure of Modern Architecture* (Van Nostrand Reinhold, 1976); Tom Wolfe, *From Bauhaus to Our House* (Farrar, Straus & Giroux, 1981); Jane Jacobs, *The Death and Life of Great American Cities* (Random House, 1961); and James Howard Kunstler, *The Geography of Nowhere* (Simon & Schuster, 1993).

If these volumes are not all readily available, the reader should inquire at the public library about the interlibrary loan service which will bring almost all books (save, perhaps, a Gutenberg Bible or a first edition of Poe's *Tamerlane*) as fast as the mail can carry them.

A number of publications deal with old buildings. *Historic Preservation* is the most visually appealing; *Old-House Journal* the most hands-on; and the *Journal of the Society of Architectural Historians* the most scholarly.

We need not always rely on the retrospective view. I have spent many fascinating hours perusing early issues of *The American Architect and Building News* (published from 1876–1908) and *The Architectural Record* (begun in 1891) to get a contemporary slant on buildings now considered venerable.

Archaeologists are sometimes suspected of gleefully waiting for buildings to be torn down so they can dig beneath them, but that is, at least in part, a bum rap. They have much to contribute toward our understanding of old houses. Unfortunately, they tend to record their results not in English but in gibberish. The next breakthrough we await is for this wonderful tale to be told in a way that will engage the reader, so that archaeological writings will not merely gather dust on untouched library shelves.

99 KELLEY LANE

ACKNOWLEDGMENTS

The author, artist, and photographer would like to express their thanks for assistance, advice, support, and friendship over the years, in ways both practical and inspirational, to the following: Henry Addis, Jim Allegro, Terri Amazeen, Shirley Ambrose, Luis Arana, Koji Ariyoshi, Tedd and Carol Arnold, Roy Barnes, Christine A. Barrett, Christopher M. Barrett, Lt. Col. Kenneth Barrett, Norton S. Baskin, Sweet Beane, Zebulon Marino Beast, Jeannie Berger, Mary Nell Black, Stanley Bond, John Bostwick, Dale Bradbury, Joel Brodsky, Louise Lastinger Brown, Kay Burtin, Roberta M. Butler, Sherry Butler, Kimmie Kim Campbell, Carlos and Davron Cardenas, Doug Carn, Lee Chellemi, Gene Claiborne, S. L. Clemens, Tom and Stephanie Coffin, LeRoy Collins, Charles Coomes, Bill Cozzens, David and June Cussen, James McBride Dabbs, Maureen Daly, Ed Davis, Regine de Toledo, Jim Dilbeck, Kenneth W. Dow, Jean Dowdy, Gilbert Driver, W. I. Drysdale, Hampton Dunn, Marguerite Lopez Dunne, Duke and Dottie Edwards, Minnie Mae Butler Edwards, Page Edwards, Gabrielle Gould Etchenique, Betty Ewing, Bill Fenton, Ann Ferran, John A. Fitzpatrick, Kat Fitzpatrick, Kevin Fitzpatrick, Liam Fitzpatrick, Mary Fitzpatrick, Molly Fitzpatrick, Ray and Wetona Fitzpatrick, Ray Fitzpatrick, Jr., Susan Fitzpatrick, William Forrester, Beverly Fowdy, Jacqueline Fretwell, Mark Fretwell, Ross Fullam, John Gadson, Betty Galipeau, Darrel Galles, Michael Gannon, Paul Gaston, Jack and Mary Jane Genung, Eddie Joyce Geyer, Clarissa Anderson Gibbs, Esther Gollobin, Gary S. Gruber, Joseph Gushanas, Jr., Rudolph Hadley, Bill and Bryanne Hamilton, George and Margaret Hamilton, Patrick S. Hamilton, Roy Hammock, Patricia Hammond, Robert W. Harper III, J. Carver Harris, Wesley L. Harris, Karen Harvey, Virginia Hassenflu, Thomas Hastings, Albert C. Hess, Sudie Cowden Hicks, Nancy Hovater, Hu Hung-fan, Zora Neale Hurston, Brian Isaacson, Errol D. Jones, Rosemary Jones, William Jovanovich, Corinne and Al Kasten, Hilda Keng, KiKi, Tom King, Silla Knox, Kimberly Lake, W. W. Law, Lorenzo Laws, Chuck Leary, Chris Lightburn, Vachel Lindsay, Margaret Lovejoy, Sister Mary Albert Lussier, Dorothy and Eugene Lyon, John and Velma Maclin, Albert Manucy, Harold Marsh, Otis A. Mason, Murphy McDaniel, Robert McGuire, William McGuire, Jeff McKenzie, Donald B. McShane, Sally Wilkowske McMillan, Bea Miner, William and Rubye Lee Moeller, Langston and Claudia Moffett, Mook's Magic Echo, Robert and Frances Neelands, Becky Hamilton Nolan, Mary Gaffney Nolan, Sudie and Hamilton Nolan, Virginia and Joseph Nolan, Nova Voce Singers, Rita O'Brien, Dannette Strange Olson, Betty Carol Parker, Idella Parker, Tiffany Parker, Rev. H. L. Patterson, X. L. Pellicer, Slade Pinkham, James Pochurek, Lynne Pochurek, Jim and Patrica Pochurek, Flossie Poe, Margo Cox Pope, Ellie Potts, Jim Quine, Heather Rainey, Melinda Rakoncay, Sally Raulerson, Marjorie Kinnan Rawlings, Lucius Rees, Corinne Richardson, Rev. F. D. Richardson, Virginia Roberts, Taryn Rodriguez-Boette, Saddle Heart, Bob Schiffer, Kris Seitz, Karen Selig, Sentry's Magic Mook, Harry Shanks, Jennie Skillman, Marsha Hamrick Slade, Elmo Slappy, Caca Smith, John L. Smith, Mary Graham Smith, Edith C. Snipes, Hilier Spokoini, Helen and Bill Stewart, Mary Elizabeth Streeter, Edward Strozier, Clarence L. Tappin, Pierre Thompson, Charles Tingley, Henry L. Twine, Frank Upchurch, Sr., Lilly Vaill, Ken and Terry Van Nortwick, Adam Van Wie, Harry Lee Vernon, Vora Vernon, Frankie Walker, Linda Brown Walker, June Weiderman, Marjorie Werner, "Miss Williamson" (Mrs. Thomas Johnson), W. Kenney Withers, Ellen Brotsky Williams, Janis Williams, Wayne Wood, C. Vann Woodward, S. Scott Young, Yao Jinrong, and the Zahra family. We would also like to thank the staffs of Chappell, Williams & Seagle, Inc., Graphics Ink, the Historic St. Augustine Preservation Board, Integroup, Inc., the St. Augustine Historical Society, the *St. Augustine Record*, the St. Johns County Public Library, and Southern Realty.

INDEX

To locate an individual building, first look up the street name. The boldface number following is the address. Numbers after that in plain type are page references.